DOCTRINAL ELEMENTS OF A CURRICULUM FRAMEWORK
*for the Development of Catechetical Materials
for Young People of High School Age*

UNITED STATES CONFERENCE OF CATHOLIC BISHOPS · WASHINGTON, D.C.

The document *Doctrinal Elements of a Curriculum Framework for the Development of Catechetical Materials for Young People of High School Age* was developed by the Committee on Evangelization and Catechesis of the United States Conference of Catholic Bishops (USCCB). It was approved by the full body of the USCCB at its November 2007 General Meeting and has been authorized for publication by the undersigned.

Msgr. David J. Malloy, STD
General Secretary, USCCB

Excerpts from the *Catechism of the Catholic Church*, second edition, copyright © 2000, Libreria Editrice Vaticana–United States Conference of Catholic Bishops, Washington, D.C. Used with permission. All rights reserved.

Scripture texts used in this work are taken from the *New American Bible,* copyright © 1991, 1986, and 1970 by the Confraternity of Christian Doctrine, Washington, DC 20017 and are used by permission of the copyright owner. All rights reserved.

Excerpts from *Vatican Council II: The Conciliar and Post Conciliar Documents* edited by Austin Flannery, OP, copyright © 1975, Costello Publishing Company, Inc., Northport, N.Y., are used with permission of the publisher, all rights reserved. No part of these excerpts may be reproduced, stored in a retrieval system, or transmitted in any form or by any means—electronic, mechanical, photocopying, recording, or otherwise—without express written permission of Costello Publishing Company.

ISBN: 978-1-60137-042-6

First printing, July 2008

Copyright © 2008, United States Conference of Catholic Bishops, Washington, D.C. All rights reserved. No part of this work may be reproduced or transmitted in any form or by any means, electronic or mechanical, including photocopying, recording, or by any information storage and retrieval system, without permission in writing from the copyright holder.

Contents

ABBREVIATIONS iv

INTRODUCTION 1

CORE CURRICULUM 2

    I. The Revelation of Jesus Christ in Scripture 2

    II. Who Is Jesus Christ? 6

    III. The Mission of Jesus Christ (The Paschal Mystery) 11

    IV. Jesus Christ's Mission Continues in the Church 15

    V. Sacraments as Privileged Encounters with Jesus Christ 20

    VI. Life in Jesus Christ 27

ELECTIVES 31

    Option A. Sacred Scripture 31

    Option B. History of the Catholic Church 35

    Option C. Living as a Disciple of Jesus Christ in Society 40

    Option D. Responding to the Call of Jesus Christ 44

    Option E. Ecumenical and Interreligious Issues 49

ABBREVIATIONS

CCC — *Catechism of the Catholic Church* (2nd ed.). Washington, DC: Libreria Editrice Vaticana–United States Conference of Catholic Bishops, 2000.

CIC — *Code of Canon Law: Latin-English Edition: New English Translation (Codex Iuris Canonici)*. Washington, DC: Canon Law Society of America, 1998.

CT — Pope John Paul II. *On Catechesis in Our Time (Catechesi Tradendae)*. Washington, DC: United States Conference of Catholic Bishops, 1987.

DV — Vatican Council II. *Dogmatic Constitution on Divine Revelation (Dei Verbum)*.

FC — Pope John Paul II. *On the Family (Familiaris Consortio)*.

GDC — Congregation for the Clergy. *General Directory for Catechesis*. Washington, DC: United States Conference of Catholic Bishops, 1998.

LG — Vatican Council II. *Dogmatic Constitution on the Church (Lumen Gentium)*. In *Vatican Council II: Volume 1: The Conciliar and Post Conciliar Documents*, edited by Austin Flannery. Northport, NY: Costello Publishing, 1996.

NAB — *New American Bible.*

NDC — United States Conference of Catholic Bishops. *National Directory for Catechesis*. Washington, DC: United States Conference of Catholic Bishops, 2005.

OS — Pope John Paul II. *On Reserving Priestly Ordination to Men Alone (Ordinatio Sacerdotalis)*. Washington, DC: United States Conference of Catholic Bishops, 1994.

RCIA — *Rite of Christian Initiation for Adults.*

UR — Vatican Council II. *Decree on Ecumenism (Unitatis Redintegratio)*.

USCCA — United States Conference of Catholic Bishops. *United States Catholic Catechism for Adults*. Washington, DC: United States Conference of Catholic Bishops, 2006.

INTRODUCTION

I have told you this so that my joy may be in you and your joy may be complete. (Jn 15:11)

"The definitive aim of catechesis is to put people not only in touch but in communion, in intimacy, with Jesus Christ" (CT, no. 5). These ends are evident in this framework—designed to guide catechetical instruction for young people of high-school age wherever and however it takes place: in Catholic high schools, in parish religious education programs, with young people schooled at home, or within the context of the catechetical instruction which should be part of every youth ministry program. The Christological centrality of this framework is designed to form the content of instruction as well as to be a vehicle for growth in one's relationship with the Lord so that each may come to know him and live according to the truth he has given to us. In this way, disciples not only participate more deeply in the life of the Church but are also better able to reach eternal life with God in Heaven.

As a framework, this document offers guidance to catechetical publishers in the creation of instructional material. Within each theme, doctrinal elements related to it are identified. The order in which the doctrinal elements within each theme are identified should not be understood to be an outline of a text or course. Rather, they are offered as building blocks that can be combined in any number of ways within that particular thematic structure and can be augmented with additional doctrinal teaching, depending on the creativity of authors and editors. In addition to aiding those creating catechetical texts and materials, this framework will also serve to aid those responsible for overseeing catechetical instruction within dioceses as well as those responsible for curriculum development or the development of assessment instruments designed to complement texts, programs, or curriculums. It is understood that implementation of a new curriculum will require time for the development of new materials as well as revision to diocesan guidelines and curricular structures within schools and religious education programs. A successful implementation will rely heavily on catechetical publishers of high-school-age materials as well as on the teachers and catechists of high-school-age young people.

The framework is designed to shape a four-year, eight-semester course of catechetical instruction. It is composed of six core semester-length subject themes with room for a diocese or school to choose two elective subject themes. It is strongly recommended that the core courses be covered in the order in which they appear in this framework. The sequence in which the core curriculum appears reflects a systematic point of view in which each course builds on a foundation laid by those that precede it. In addition, some national uniformity in catechetical instruction on the high-school-age level would be a benefit in the modern mobile society. Five possible elective themes appear as part of this framework. Normally, the elective themes should appear either as one in the third year and one in the fourth year or both in the fourth year.

Since this is a framework and not a tool for direct instruction, the doctrines and topics designated are not necessarily defined or completely developed. Such detail will be present in the catechetical texts and materials that will be developed on the basis of this framework. It is expected that after developing new materials, publishing houses will submit them for a review as to their conformity with the *Catechism of the Catholic Church*. The process of that review will ensure that the materials authentically and completely define and present the teaching of the Church.

In addition to providing guidance about the doctrinal content of catechetical instruction for high-school-age young people, this framework is also designed to help those same young people develop the necessary skills to answer or address the real questions that they face in life and in their Catholic faith. Within each theme, including the electives, there is a section titled "Challenges," which raises examples of these questions and provides direction for ways to answer them. This element is designed to give catechetical instruction for high-school-age young people an apologetical component. Publishers and teachers or catechists are to strive to provide for a catechetical instruction and formation that is imbued with an apologetical approach. Challenges that appear under one particular theme can also apply to other themes in the framework, and such application is encouraged. The identification and inclusion of additional challenges by publishers and by teachers or catechists to achieve this goal is also encouraged.

CORE CURRICULUM

I. The Revelation of Jesus Christ in Scripture

The purpose of this course is to give students a general knowledge and appreciation of the Sacred Scriptures. Through their study of the Bible they will come to encounter the living Word of God, Jesus Christ. In the course they will learn about the Bible, authored by God through Inspiration, and its value to people throughout the world. If they have not been taught this earlier, they will learn how to read the Bible and will become familiar with the major sections of the Bible and the books included in each section. The students will pay particular attention to the Gospels, where they may grow to know and love Jesus Christ more personally.

I. How Do We Know About God?

A. The thirst and desire for God (*Catechism of the Catholic Church* [CCC], nos. 27-30, 44-45, 1718).
   1. Within all people there is a longing for God.
   2. That longing itself is from God, who desires and initiates a relationship with each person.
   3. Only in God can lasting joy and peace be found in this life and in the next.

B. God revealed in many ways.
   1. Natural Revelation (CCC, nos. 32-34).
      a. Natural Revelation attested to in Sacred Scripture (CCC, no. 32).
         1) Old Testament references, including Genesis and Wisdom.
         2) Paul's Letter to the Romans.
      b. Patristic testimony (CCC, no. 32).
      c. Scholastic theology's arguments for the existence of God (CCC, nos. 31, 34).
         1) St. Thomas Aquinas and the five proofs for the existence of God.
      d. Vatican I: we can grasp with certainty the existence of God through human reason (CCC, nos. 36-38, 46-47).
      e. Contemporary arguments based on the human person's opening to truth, beauty, moral goodness, freedom, voice of conscience (CCC, no. 33).
   2. Divine Revelation.
      a. Definition/meaning (CCC, nos. 50-53, 68-69).
      b. Scripture as a divinely inspired record of God's Revelation in history (CCC, nos. 54-64, 70-72).
         1) Abraham, Isaac, Jacob (CCC, nos. 59, 145, 147).
         2) Moses (CCC, no. 61).
         3) Old Testament prophets (CCC, nos. 61-64, 522).
         4) Wisdom literature.
         5) Preparation through John the Baptist (CCC, nos. 523, 717-720).
      c. Jesus Christ, the first and the last, the definitive Word of Revelation, the one to whom all Scripture bears witness, is God's only Son (CCC, nos. 65-67, 73, 101-104, 134, 423).
   3. The transmission of Divine Revelation (CCC, nos. 74-95).
      a. Apostolic Tradition (CCC, nos. 74-79, 96).
      b. The relationship between Tradition and Sacred Scripture (CCC, nos. 80-83, 97).
      c. The Deposit of Faith and the role of the Church (CCC, nos. 84-95, 98-100).

II. About Sacred Scripture

A. Divine Inspiration.
   1. Inspiration is the gift of the Holy Spirit by which a human author was able to write a biblical book which really has God as the author and which teaches faithfully and without error the saving truth that God willed to be consigned to us for our salvation (CCC, nos. 105, 135).
   2. Since God inspired the biblical writers, he is the author of Scripture (CCC, nos. 105-106, 136).
   3. Because the human authors needed to use the language and thinking of their time, we need to study the conditions and use of language in the context of their time and understand what they intended to communicate, remembering that these human authors might not have been conscious of the deeper implications of what God wanted to communicate (CCC, nos. 106, 108-114).
   4. The Bible is inerrant in matters of Revelation and faith: because God is the author of Scripture, all the religious truths that God intends to reveal

concerning our salvation are true; this attribute is called "inerrancy" (see DV, no. 11; CCC, no. 107).
	5. The Bible is a sacred text for Christians; it contains in the Old Testament writings sacred to the Jews.
B. How the Bible came to be.
	1. Oral tradition and its role (CCC, nos. 76, 126).
	2. Development of the written books (CCC, nos. 76, 106).
	3. Setting the canon of Scripture (CCC, no. 120).
		a. Apostolic Tradition is the basis for which books the Church included (CCC, nos. 120, 138).
		b. Sometimes other criteria came into play, e.g., the Gnostic gospels were rejected in part because they did not include or shied away from the suffering and Death of Jesus.
		c. Local Councils of Hippo (AD 393) and Carthage (AD 397).
		d. Ecumenical Council of Trent (AD 1545-1563).
	4. Translations of Scripture.
C. Sacred Scripture in the life of the Church.
	1. Importance of Sacred Scripture (CCC, nos. 131, 133, 141).
	2. Study of Sacred Scripture (CCC, no. 132).
	3. Scripture and prayer.
		a. Liturgy of the Hours (CCC, nos. 1176-1177).
		b. Scripture at Mass and other liturgies (CCC, nos. 103, 1096, 1100, 1184, 1190, 1349).
		c. The psalms and the Our Father are biblical prayers shared by all Christians (CCC, nos. 2585ff., 2759ff.).
		d. *Lectio divina*: a meditative, prayerful approach to Scripture (CCC, nos. 1177, 2708).
		e. Scripture as basis for individual prayer and for prayer within small Christian communities and other parish, school, or local gatherings (CCC, nos. 2653-2654).

III. Understanding Scripture

A. Authentic interpretation of the Bible is the responsibility of the teaching office of the Church (CCC, nos. 85-87, 100).
	1. *Divino Afflante Spiritu* (Pius XII, 1943; permitted limited use of modern methods of biblical criticism).
	2. *Dei Verbum* (DV) (Vatican II, 1965; Church teaching on Revelation).
	3. Pontifical Biblical Commission, *Interpretation of the Bible in the Church*, 1993, nos. 5-19.
B. Criteria for interpreting the Sacred Scripture (CCC, nos. 109-114, 137).
	1. Read and interpret Sacred Scripture within the tradition and teaching of the Church.
	2. Give attention both to what the human authors intended to say and to what God reveals to us by their words.
	3. Take into account the conditions of the time when it was written and the culture where it was written.
	4. Read and interpret Sacred Scripture in the light of the same Holy Spirit by whom it was written (DV, nos. 12-13).
	5. Read and interpret each part of Sacred Scripture with an awareness and understanding of the unity of the content and teaching of the entire Bible.
	6. Be attentive to the analogy of faith, that is, the unity that exists in all Church teaching.
C. Senses of Scripture (CCC, nos. 115, 118-119).
	1. The literal sense: the meaning conveyed by the words of Scripture and discovered by exegesis (CCC, nos. 109-110, 116).
	2. The spiritual sense (CCC, no. 117).
		a. Allegorical sense: recognizing the significance of events in the Bible as they relate to Christ.
		b. Moral sense: Scripture teaches us and encourages us how to live and act.
		c. Anagogical sense: Scripture speaks to us of eternal realities.
D. The Bible in relation to science and history (CCC, nos. 37, 159, 1960).
	1. The Church teaches us how to relate truths of faith to science.
	2. There can be no conflict between religious truth and scientific and historical truth (CCC, no. 159).
	3. The difference between the Catholic understanding of Scripture and that of those who interpret the Bible in an overly literalist, fundamentalist way or with an approach limited to a symbolic understanding.
E. Ancillary approaches to Scripture.
	1. Research done by scholars' critiques of Scripture's texts, history, editing, etc.
	2. Biblical archaeology: discoveries of Dead Sea Scrolls, Nag Hammadi, targums, and other authentic ancient texts.
	3. The forms of literature in the Bible.

IV. Overview of the Bible

A. Old Testament (CCC, nos. 121-123, 138).
 1. This is the name given to the forty-six books which make up the first part of the Bible and record salvation history prior to the coming of the Savior, Jesus Christ (CCC, no. 120).
    a. Many Protestant Bibles have only thirty-nine books in the Old Testament; other Protestant Bibles contain the additional seven, referring to them as "deuterocanonical."
    b. Catholics rely on the Greek version of the Old Testament for their Bible, while Protestants tend to rely on a Hebrew version.
 2. It is called the "Old" Testament because it relates God's teaching and actions prior to the coming of Jesus Christ, who is the fullness of Revelation. It also focuses on the covenant God made with the Jewish people, which is called the "Old Covenant" to distinguish it from the New Covenant made by Jesus Christ (CCC, nos. 121-123).
 3. The Old Testament contains the Pentateuch, the Historical books, the Wisdom books, and the Prophetic books.

B. New Testament (CCC, nos. 120, 124-127).
 1. This is the name given to those twenty-seven books which compose the second part of the Bible and which focus on the life and teachings of Jesus Christ and some writings of the early Church.
 2. The New Testament is composed of the Gospels, the Acts of the Apostles, the Epistles or Letters, and the book of Revelation.

C. The unity of the Old Testament and the New Testament (CCC, nos. 124-125, 128-130, 140).

V. The Gospels

A. The Gospels occupy the central place in Scripture (CCC, nos. 125, 139).
 1. They proclaim the Good News of Jesus Christ, the Word of God, the definitive Revelation of God.
 2. The Gospels contain a record of the life of Jesus Christ and of his teachings and redeeming work.
 3. The Gospels lead us to accept Jesus Christ in faith and apply his teachings to our lives.

B. Three stages in the formation of the Gospels (CCC, no. 126).

C. The Synoptic Gospels: Matthew, Mark, and Luke.
 1. Approximate dates for each Gospel.
 2. What is known about each of these three evangelists.
 3. The churches for whom Matthew, Mark, and Luke wrote.
 4. The contents of the Synoptic Gospels (CCC, nos. 512-667).
    a. Infancy narratives in Matthew and Luke.
    b. The Baptism of Jesus.
    c. The Temptation of Jesus.
    d. Sermon on the Mount in Matthew; Sermon on the Plain in Luke.
    e. Jesus' teaching, including the parables.
    f. The miracles.
    g. Last Supper, the Passion, Death, Resurrection, Ascension (CCC, nos. 1329, 1337, 1366, 1323, 1412, 1521-1522, 1532, 1708, 1992, 2020).

D. The Gospel of John.
 1. Approximate date of the Gospel and churches for which John wrote.
 2. What is known about John.
 3. The content of the Gospel of John.
    a. The Prologue (CCC, nos. 241, 291).
    b. John uses Christ's dialogues and personal testimony and is more mystical (CCC, nos. 547-550).
    c. John treats miracles as signs of Christ's glory/divinity—flows from John 1:14.
    d. The Bread of Life discourse (Jn 6).
    e. Christ's Last Supper discourse and priestly prayer.
    f. The Passion, Death, Resurrection.

VI. Challenges

A. Is it true that Catholics do not use or read the Bible?
 1. No. Catholics use the Bible regularly. The Bible or Scripture is an integral part of Catholic prayer life, forming part of every Mass, every sacramental celebration, and the official daily prayer of the Church—the Liturgy of the Hours (CCC, nos. 141, 1190).
 2. The Church urges Catholics to use the Bible in personal prayer (CCC, nos. 2653-2654).
 3. Scripture study and prayer groups using Scripture are a common part of parish life.
 4. In the fourth century, St. Jerome said that "ignorance of the Scriptures is ignorance of Christ"; this underlines the importance of Scripture in the life of the Church (CCC, no. 133).

B. Isn't the Bible just another piece of literature?
   1. No. While Scripture contains various types of literary forms and genres, it is more than just literature. It is the inspired Word of God (CCC, no. 135).
   2. Since it is not just another piece of literature, Scripture cannot be either read or understood merely in the same way as other literature (CCC, no. 108).
   3. Scripture always needs to be read or interpreted in the light of the Holy Spirit and under the direction of the Church (CCC, nos. 100, 111, 119, 137).

C. Is the Bible always literally true?
   1. It depends on what one means by "literally." The Church does not always propose a literalist or fundamentalist approach to Scripture but rather a contextualist approach. The Church teaches that all of Scripture is true on matters pertaining to religious and salvific teaching because it is inspired by God for that purpose (CCC, nos. 107, 116).
   2. The Bible has a definite historic basis for events recounted in both the Old and the New Testaments; the Church particularly upholds the historicity of the Gospels (CCC, no. 126). However, the Church does not claim that the Bible's purpose is to present scientific or historical facts (CCC, no. 107).
   3. The Church gives guidelines for interpretation of Sacred Scripture (see earlier in outline).

D. Isn't the Bible about the past? Why do people today think it applies to them?
   1. While the Bible contains history, stories, and teaching about events in the past, Scripture is the living Word of God. While the content is rooted in particular moments in history, the message is timeless and universal.
   2. God continues to speak to us through Scripture; this is why the liturgies of the Church always contain Scripture and why personal prayer focused on Scripture is vital.

E. Why do Catholics maintain beliefs and practices that are not in the Bible?
   1. The Bible is not the sole means that God chose to hand on the truths of Revelation. Scripture and Tradition are the two complementary ways Revelation is passed down (CCC, nos. 80, 97).
   2. There are teachings that come through Tradition that are not explicitly found in Scripture. However, nothing taught through Tradition ever contradicts Scripture since both come from Christ through the Apostles (CCC, no. 82).
   3. Apostolic Tradition refers to those things that Jesus taught to the Apostles and early disciples, which were passed down to us at first by word of mouth and were only written down later. We identify these beliefs as coming from Tradition and understand that this Tradition is part of God's Revelation to us (CCC, no. 83).

F. Why do some people try to change what the Church teaches about Jesus Christ?
   1. People have tried to change teaching about Christ for many different reasons. Sometimes it is to justify their particular belief or lack of belief. Sometimes it has been out of sincere but misguided or misinformed efforts to try to explain mysteries about Jesus Christ or God's Revelation.
   2. In the early history of the Church, there were a number of heresies about Jesus Christ which arose when people tried to explain the mystery of who he was and is. An example of this is the Arian heresy, which denied the full divinity of Christ.
   3. Sometimes people did not like what Jesus taught or did or what happened to him. There were a number of "gospels" written, which the Church, under the guidance of the Holy Spirit, recognized as not authentic. Some of these gospels shied away from teaching the Incarnation, suffering, Death, and Resurrection of Jesus.
   4. In modern times, there are individuals and groups who try to explain in natural scientific terms the miracles of Jesus, thus undermining his divinity.

II. Who Is Jesus Christ?

The purpose of this course is to introduce students to the mystery of Jesus Christ, the living Word of God, the Second Person of the Blessed Trinity. In this course students will understand that Jesus Christ is the ultimate Revelation to us from God. In learning about who he is, the students will also learn who he calls them to be.

I. God and Revelation

A. Revelation: God's gift of himself.
   1. Divine Revelation (CCC, nos. 50-73).
      a. Definition/meaning.
      b. The divine plan is disclosed—salvation history.
   2. Scripture, Tradition, and the Deposit of Faith (CCC, nos. 74-100, 103-108, 134-135).
      a. Definitions/meanings.
      b. Scripture is the inspired record of God's Revelation in history.
      c. Tradition is the living transmission of the message of the Gospel in the Church.
B. Faith: the response to God's self-Revelation.
   1. What is faith in general (CCC, nos. 143-144, 153-165)?
      a. A grace that enables an assent of mind, heart, and will (CCC, no. 143).
      b. Willingness to believe and trust in what God has communicated to us.
      c. Relationship with God: Father, Son, and Holy Spirit (CCC, nos. 150-152).
   2. Faith in Jesus Christ leads to discipleship (CCC, nos. 520, 546, 562, 654, 1533).
      a. Recognition and acceptance of him as the Son of God who died to save us from our sins (CCC, no. 1248).
      b. Willingness to believe and trust in what Jesus has taught us about the Triune God, about ourselves, and about how to live (CCC, nos. 915, 1693, 1816, 1823, 1986, 2262, 2347, 2427, 2466, 2612).
      c. This faith has practical implications for daily life and one's relationship with Christ (CCC, no. 908).
      d. Involves active participation in the Church community and working to spread the faith by word and example.
   3. The relationship between faith and religion (CCC, nos. 2084, 2135).
      a. Religion refers to a set of beliefs and practices followed by those committed to the service and worship of God.
      b. Faith is different from religion.
   4. The fullness of Revelation is reflected in the life and teaching of the Catholic Church (CCC, nos. 748-870).
      a. The Church was founded by Jesus Christ (CCC, nos. 811-812).
      b. Church is the Body of Christ in the world.
      c. The Church is a unity of one faith in one Lord through one Baptism (CCC, nos. 813-16).
      d. The Magisterium guards and hands on the deposit of faith and is entrusted with the authentic interpretation of Revelation (CCC, nos. 880-896).

II. Jesus Christ's Revelation About God

A. Son of God from all eternity and Son of Mary from the moment of the Incarnation (CCC, nos. 486, 496, 487, 501, 721-730).
   1. Mystery of the Incarnation: Emmanuel (God-is-with-us) (Jn 3:16-17; CCC, no. 484).
      a. Jesus Christ is the Logos, the Word of God, the fulfillment of God's promise to Adam and Eve and to the people of ancient Israel (CCC, nos. 761-762).
      b. Christ continues his presence in the world through the Church (CCC, nos. 732, 737-739, 747).
      c. All events of Christ's life are worthy of reflection and imitation (see Gospel accounts).
B. The Revelation of Jesus about God (Jn 14:9).
   1. God is Trinity: one in three Divine Persons (CCC, no. 234).
      a. This is the central mystery of our faith (CCC, nos. 235-237).

b. The Divine Persons are distinct from one another (CCC, no. 254).
   c. The Divine Persons are relative to one another; each is God whole and entire; all three persons share the same attributes, i.e., all-loving, eternal, etc. (CCC, nos. 255-256).
   d. Each Divine Person shows forth what is proper to him, especially in the Incarnation and the gift of the Holy Spirit (CCC, nos. 258, 267).
  2. God is the Father: Jesus Christ's Father and our Father.
     a. Jesus teaches us that God is loving, caring, healing, forgiving, true, just.
     b. God the Father's love is faithful and eternal.
C. The Three Divine Persons of the Trinity.
  1. The First Person of the Trinity: God the Father (CCC, nos. 238-242).
     a. God the Father is the source of all that is, visible and invisible.
     b. God is Father in relation to the Son from all eternity (CCC, no. 240).
     c. God is Father to all those baptized as his adopted sons and daughters through and in the Son (CCC, nos. 232-233, 249).
     d. God the Father of mercy also cares for the unbaptized (CCC, nos. 1257, 1260-1261).
  2. The Second Person of the Trinity: God the Son.
     a. Jesus Christ is eternally begotten and incarnate in time (CCC, nos. 461, 422).
     b. Son of God, true God, consubstantial with the Father (CCC, no. 252).
     c. Son of Mary, true man; the perfection of who we are created to be (CCC, nos. 430, 456-469, 484-487).
     d. Savior and Redeemer (CCC, nos. 517, 651-658).
  3. The Third Person of the Trinity: the Holy Spirit, the Lord and giver of life (CCC, nos. 243-248).
     a. Eternally proceeding from the Father and the Son (CCC, no. 687).
     b. Only fully revealed by Jesus (CCC, nos. 689-690, 727-730).
     c. Sanctifier of the Church and her members, e.g., gifts and fruits of the Holy Spirit (CCC, nos. 32, 731-741, 1830-1832).
  4. The development of Trinitarian theology in the early councils of the Church (CCC, nos. 245-248).
     a. The struggles of the Church to maintain apostolic faith in light of Christological controversies and heresies (CCC, nos. 249-252).
     b. Church teaching articulated to battle Gnosticism, Arianism, Nestorianism, Monophysitism (CCC, nos. 464-469).
  5. Unique role of Mary, the Mother of God.
     a. The Annunciation and Mary's "yes" (CCC, nos. 484-487).
     b. An unparalleled recipient of God's grace: Immaculate Conception; Assumption (CCC, nos. 490-494, 966).
     c. Mary is ever-virgin (CCC, nos. 499-507).
        1) Explain references in the Gospels to the brothers and sisters of Jesus (CCC, nos. 500-501).
     d. Mary is the Mother of the Church (CCC, no. 507).
     e. Mary is the first disciple.

III. The Mystery of the Incarnation

A. Jesus Christ is fully God and fully man (CCC, nos. 464-469).
  1. Jesus Christ, a Divine Person, is truly the Son of God, who, without ceasing to be God and Lord, became man and our brother (CCC, no. 469).
  2. Jesus Christ took on a human nature. The eternal Son of God incarnate worked with human hands; he thought with a human mind. He acted with a human will, and with a human heart he loved. He was like us in all things except sin (CCC, no. 470). Man's creator has become man (CCC, no. 526).
  3. Jesus showed his humanity in every event of his human life (CCC, nos. 512-534):
     a. In his family life, his friendships, and his socialization with others we see him experience human joy and happiness and demonstrate human virtues.
     b. Through things such as hunger and thirst in the desert, temptation by the Devil, grief at the death of Lazarus, agony in the Garden of Gethsemane, and his Death on the Cross, we know that he also experienced pain, suffering, and sorrow. In his human encounter with the sick and the outcast, he personified compassion (CCC, no. 538).
  4. The unity of the two natures in the one Person is called the "hypostatic union" (CCC, no. 468).

IV. Jesus Christ Teaches Us About Ourselves

A. Jesus embodies what has been revealed in and through creation.
   1. God created the human person in his image and likeness; male and female he created them. This is why we must respect the dignity of all people (CCC, nos. 1700-1709).
   2. To be fully human means to fully accept and become the person God created us to be, a human person endowed with special gifts which reflect God: immortality, intellect, free will, the ability to love (CCC, nos. 356-358, 1702-1706).
   3. The Incarnation affirms that we are created as good, but in need of salvation, and are meant for eternal glory with God. The Incarnation also describes how God continues to work out our sanctification in the world, e.g., Church, sacraments, priesthood (CCC, nos. 461-469).
   4. God has entrusted his creation to us; we are stewards charged with procreating and protecting life and using the rest of creation respectfully (CCC, nos. 287, 354).

B. Jesus Christ redeems us and gives us his grace so that we can choose the good according to God's will and resist sin and its effects (CCC, nos. 1705, 1708-1709).
   1. Jesus invites us to believe in him, to invite him into our hearts, and to follow him and his teaching as the path that leads to life, for he is "the way, the truth, and the life" and is worthy of our belief, adoration, and love (CCC, nos. 1741-1742).
   2. He reveals the way to repentance and conversion, teaching us to leave sin behind and to live a new life in him; he gives us the spiritual power and grace to overcome evil; he also teaches us about God's forgiveness (CCC, nos. 1847-1848).
   3. He teaches us how to be single-hearted in our desire for God, to offset the disordered affections and divided hearts with which we live (CCC, nos. 1716-1717).

C. Jesus Christ reveals the Father to us, who we are, and our call to holiness.
   1. By becoming man, and by his Death and Resurrection, Jesus Christ unites us to God (CCC, nos. 461-464).
   2. We become the free adopted children of the Father through Baptism (Gal 4; CCC, nos. 1265-1270).
   3. We are conformed to Christ and can grow in holiness and goodness.
      a. Lessons from the Sermon on the Mount (Mt 5–7; CCC, nos. 1716-1724).
      b. Parables and other teaching of Jesus Christ (CCC, no. 546).
      c. "Good teacher, what must I do to inherit eternal life?" (Mk 10:17-22).
      d. The Two Great Commandments: love of God and love of neighbor (CCC, nos. 2083-2557).
      e. Teaching about the final judgment (Mt 25: 31-46; CCC, nos. 544, 1033, 1373, 2447, 2831).
   4. He teaches us to pray and teaches us through prayer (CCC, nos. 2607-2615).
      a. In the Gospels, the Lord Jesus teaches us about prayer:
         1) Going off by himself to pray teaches us the importance of finding time for prayer (Mk 1:35, 6:46; Lk 5:16).
         2) Jesus Christ teaches his Apostles and disciples to pray (Mt 7:7-11; CCC, no. 2609).
         3) The Lord Jesus teaches the importance of perseverance in prayer (Lk 11:5-13, 18:1-8; CCC, nos. 2729-2737, 2742-2745).
      b. Jesus Christ teaches us through prayer:
         1) The Lord Jesus teaches us to approach prayer with humility and a sense of need (Lk 18:9-14).
         2) God is our Father, whom we approach through prayer (Mt 6:9-13; Lk 11:2-4; CCC, nos. 2759ff.).
         3) Jesus Christ intercedes for us (Jn 14:13, 16:24; CCC, nos. 2665-2669).
   5. Jesus sends out his disciples to evangelize (Lk 10: 1-20; Mt 28:16-20; CCC, nos. 861, 905).

D. Jesus also tells us of the goal in this life and of the end of life.
   1. The Communion of Saints (CCC, nos. 948, 957, 960, 1474).
   2. Four last things.
      a. Death (CCC, nos. 992, 996, 1007, 1010-1014, 2299).
      b. Judgment: particular and final (CCC, nos. 677-679, 1021, 1038-1041).
         1) Purgatory (CCC, nos. 1030-1032).
      c. Heaven (CCC, nos. 1023-1029).
      d. Hell (CCC, nos. 1033-1037).

V. Challenges

A. How can we know God really exists?

1. Even without the Bible and Divine Revelation, we can know God really exists through reason and through experience (CCC, nos. 36-39, 50, 156-159).

2. By looking around at creation, reason and experience can point to God's existence (CCC, nos. 156-159).

   a. The order and beauty of the natural world point to God as the origin and Creator of the universe (CCC, no. 295).

   b. Creation did not happen by chance; throughout history the Church has taught that someone had to be behind it, and that someone is God (CCC, nos. 156, 295).

   c. The natural law written upon each person's heart and the longing for God that each person has also point to God's existence (CCC, nos. 1954-1960).

3. Reason and experience can also teach us to accept the word of other believers (CCC, no. 39).

   a. God's Revelation comes down to us through Scripture and Tradition (CCC, nos. 50-53, 74-83).

   b. The testimony and witness of others who have gone before us: people whose stories appear in the Bible; Apostles, saints, and martyrs (CCC, nos. 823, 828, 857, 946, 1258, 2473).

   c. The faith of people we know today: the pope and the bishops in union with him; priests and deacons; parents, grandparents, and other family members; teachers and catechists; the witness of fellow Catholics as well as the witness of non-Catholic believers (CCC, nos. 85, 1655-1658).

4. We can also know God exists through faith. For those who do believe, through faith as well as prayer and grace, they can grow in the knowledge and experience of the reality of God and his existence (CCC, nos. 143, 153-159).

B. There are some who see human suffering and conclude that God does not care about us. Why do we say that he loves us deeply (CCC, nos. 1503-1505, 1681, 1808)?

1. We say God loves us deeply, even in the midst of suffering, because he reveals his love to us in many ways, especially in Christ's taking our suffering upon himself for our sake (CCC, no. 1505).

   a. He shows us his love in creation (CCC, no. 54).

      1) God created the world entirely out of love and not out of necessity (CCC, no. 295).

      2) God created human beings in his image and likeness with the ability to give and receive love (CCC, nos. 1700-1706).

   b. The suffering and Death of Jesus Christ shows and proves that love (CCC, nos. 599-623).

      1) God sent his Son to redeem everyone from sin so that all can share a life of love eternally with him (Jn 3:16-17; CCC, nos. 599-605).

      2) Jesus lives now and establishes a relationship with each and every one of us, particularly through the sacramental life of the Church (CCC, nos. 662-664, 1084-1090).

      3) God continually calls us to union with him in his Son through the Holy Spirit by means of a life of holiness (CCC, nos. 1091-1109).

   c. God helps us know and sense his love through the people and events of our lives (CCC, nos. 897-913, 1069).

2. We also know of his love because he tells us of his loving plan to save us.

   a. He tells us in Scripture, the living Word of God (CCC, nos. 80-82).

   b. He also tells us through the liturgy of the Church, speaking to us in the Scripture and giving himself to us in the sacraments, especially the Eucharist (CCC, nos. 1067, 1324-1327).

   c. He tells us through the Church (CCC, nos. 785-786).

C. How can people say that God is good if suffering and evil are present in the world?

1. Suffering that exists in the world is not something caused by God or sent by God; God only brings about what is good for he is goodness itself. When there is evil and suffering, God does not cause it, but sometimes he does permit it for reasons we cannot now know or understand (CCC, nos. 1500-1501).

2. Evil is a reality and a mystery, that is, it is hard to understand the why of it (CCC, nos. 309-314). Some evil and suffering are a result of the work of the Devil or Satan (CCC, no. 395).

3. Some suffering is the result of human sin and is not from God. It was God who gave us free will; sin is the result of the misuse of this gift (CCC, nos. 1849, 1852-1853).

4. The Passion and Death of Jesus can help us to see beyond suffering and remind us that God is present with us in our suffering, pain, and death; our own personal suffering when united to Jesus' suffering becomes redemptive for ourselves and others (CCC, no. 1851).
5. The Scriptures try to help us understand suffering: the psalms, the story of Job, and the prophets offer insights and consolation. In particular, the Resurrection of Jesus can help us see beyond suffering to hope and to eternal life (CCC, nos. 638-655).
6. We need to remember that God always wants what is best for us (CCC, nos. 374-379).
7. Natural disasters can be understood in part as a result of Original Sin (CCC, no. 400) and also because the world is in a state of journeying toward ultimate perfection (CCC, no. 310); they are not signs of God's displeasure or punishment.

D. Does God really want us to be happy?
1. Yes. From the beginning of Creation, God has created us to be happy both in this world and in the next and has shown us the ways to be truly happy. Unhappiness was caused by people themselves when they did not or would not listen to him (CCC, nos. 374-379).
2. God sent his only Son, Jesus Christ, so that we might be saved (Jn 3:16); that confident hope is the cause for happiness in spite of suffering (CCC, nos. 599-605).
3. Jesus Christ taught us all he did so that we might share in his joy (Jn 15:11), which shows us again his desire for our happiness (CCC, nos. 736, 1832).
4. The blueprint for true discipleship and happiness is found in Christ's teaching of the Beatitudes (Mt 5:2-10; CCC, nos. 1716-1718).
5. True joy is the mark of followers of Christ (Phil 4:4; CCC, no. 1832).
6. Jesus established his Church to help people find true happiness and joy (CCC, no. 1832).

E. There are some who dismiss God's Revelation and say that the beliefs and doctrines taught by the Church have been made up by members of the Church. How can we be sure that what the Catholic Church teaches has come from God?
1. We can be sure that what the Church teaches has come from God because of Apostolic Tradition and Apostolic Succession (CCC, nos. 888-892, 861-862, 858-860).
   a. What was revealed in and through Jesus Christ was entrusted to St. Peter and the Apostles, who were taught directly by Jesus. They in turn passed on those beliefs through those who succeeded them (CCC, nos. 81, 84).
   b. Through the centuries, the popes and bishops, the successors of St. Peter and the Apostles, have carefully transmitted to the generations whom they shepherd the truths revealed and taught by Jesus Christ (CCC, nos. 96, 171, 173, 815).
   c. Jesus Christ promised his Apostles that he would be with the Church until the end of time (Mt 28:20).
2. Christ has also given the Church a share in his own infallibility (CCC, nos. 889-892).

F. How do we as Catholics answer questions about the Blessed Virgin Mary and her role in the life and prayer of the Church (CCC, nos. 148, 484-511, 721-726, 773, 963-972, 829)?
1. Questions about why Catholics pray to Mary.
   a. Catholics do not worship Mary; worship belongs to God alone. They venerate Mary and the saints.
   b. Mary does not have the power to answer prayers on her own; God alone has that power.
   c. Prayers to Mary are asking for her intercessory help.
      1) Since Mary is already in Heaven, she will know better than we how to offer praise and prayer to God.
      2) When people pray to the Blessed Mother they are asking her in turn to offer the same prayer for them to God.
      3) When Mary and the saints were on earth, they cooperated with God to do good for others; so now from their place in Heaven they continue to cooperate with God by doing good for others who are in need on earth and in Purgatory.
2. Questions about references in the Gospels to the brothers and sisters of Jesus.
   a. From the earliest days of the Church, Mary has been revered as ever-virgin; she was a virgin before Jesus' birth and remained a virgin afterward.
   b. It is not clear who the "brothers and sisters" of Jesus are.
      1) At the time Jesus lived, the designation "brother and sister" also referred to cousins and sometimes even close neighbors.

III. The Mission of Jesus Christ (The Paschal Mystery)

The purpose of this course is to help students understand all that God has done for us through his Son, Jesus Christ. Through this course of study, students will learn that for all eternity, God has planned for us to share eternal happiness with him, which is accomplished through the redemption Christ won for us. Students will learn that they share in this redemption only in and through Jesus Christ. They will also be introduced to what it means to be a disciple of Christ and what life as a disciple entails.

I. The Goodness of Creation and Our Fall from Grace

A. The Creation of the World and our first parents (CCC, nos. 54, 279-282).
  1. Revelation as found in the book of Genesis.
     a. Understanding literary forms in Scripture (CCC, no. 289).
     b. Genesis 1–11 conveys religious truth rather than science (CCC, nos. 283-289).
     c. The book reveals truth about which science and history can only speculate.
     d. Scripture's use of figurative and symbolic language in Genesis 1–11 (CCC, nos. 362, 375, 390, 396).
  2. The Trinitarian God is the Creator of all; all creation reflects the glory of God (CCC, nos. 290-295, 301).
  3. God created all that is, seen and unseen.
     a. Unseen or invisible world: angels (CCC, nos. 325-336).
     b. Seen or visible world (CCC, nos. 349-357).
  4. Human beings as the summit of creation.
     a. Created in the image and likeness of God (CCC, nos. 356-359, 1700-1706).
        1) God made them male and female (CCC, nos. 369-373, 1605, 1702, 2331).
        2) Dignity of both men and women: similarities and differences (CCC, nos. 2333-2336).
        3) Contributions to the world and to the Church (CCC, nos. 2346-2347).
     b. Human persons are a body-soul unity; this reflects the physical and spiritual realities in the world (CCC, nos. 356-368).
  5. God's plan: original holiness and original justice (CCC, nos. 374-379).

B. The fall from grace: Original Sin (Gn 3; Rom 5:12; CCC, nos. 55, 309-314, 385-390, 1707).
  1. The full meaning of the doctrine of Original Sin is revealed only in the light of the Death and Resurrection of Jesus. It is essential to belief in the mystery of Christ. The whole of human history is marked by the sin of the first parents (CCC, no. 1708).
  2. The fall of the angels (CCC, nos. 391-395).
  3. The rebellion of Adam and Eve and its consequences.
     a. The rebellion of Adam and Eve was a sin of disobedience toward God, a rejection of a God-centered life and the choice of a self-centered life (CCC, nos. 396-398).
     b. The consequences of Adam and Eve's sin: loss of paradise, original grace, original holiness, and original justice (CCC, nos. 399-401).
     c. Original Sin and its consequences for all: suffering, death, a tendency toward sin, need for salvation (CCC, nos. 402-409).

II. The Promise of a Messiah

A. The first prophecy of the Messiah, God's promise to redeem the world (Gn 3:15; CCC, no. 410).
  1. God's immediate response to Adam and Eve's sin is to promise redemption; this is the *Proto-Evangelium*, the first announcement of the Good News (CCC, nos. 410-412).
  2. Promise endures despite the escalation of sin (the Book of Genesis: the murder of Abel, the Tower of Babel, the Flood) (CCC, nos. 55-64).

B. Longing for the fulfillment of the promise (CCC, nos. 121-123).
  1. God's covenants with Old Testament peoples (CCC, nos. 129-130).

a. The covenants are solemn commitments between God and human beings (CCC, no. 56).
b. God made a covenant with Noah, with Abraham, and with Moses (CCC, nos. 56-64).
c. Each of these covenants foreshadows the Paschal Mystery (CCC, no. 129).
2. The people of ancient Israel entrusted with knowledge of God's promise.
3. Judges, kings, and prophets: reminding the people of ancient Israel about the promise.
4. The promise to David.
5. The "suffering servant" passages in Isaiah.

C. The promise of redemption is fulfilled in Jesus (CCC, nos. 422-451).
1. The Gospels recognize Jesus as the fulfillment of the promise.
   a. The Annunciation: Mary's "yes" to God, her consent to be the Mother of God (*Theotokos*) (Lk 1:38; CCC, nos. 484-489).
   b. The dream of St. Joseph; the role of St. Joseph in the life of Jesus and Mary (CCC, nos. 496-507).
   c. The Gospels apply the ancient prophesies to Jesus (CCC, nos. 522-524).
2. Why the Word became flesh (the Incarnation) (CCC, nos. 525-528, 456-478).
   a. To save us by reconciling us with God, who loved us and sent his Son to be the expiation for our sins (CCC, no. 457).
   b. That we might come to know the depth of God's love for us (CCC, no. 458).
   c. To be our model of holiness (CCC, no. 459).
   d. To make us partakers of the divine nature (CCC, nos. 457-460).
   e. To destroy the power of the Devil (1 Jn 3:8).
3. Christ's whole life was a mystery of redemption (CCC, nos. 535-618).
   a. By becoming poor he enriched us with his poverty.
   b. In his hidden life his obedience atoned for our disobedience.
   c. In his preached word he purified our consciences.
   d. In his compassion and in his healings and exorcisms he bore our infirmities.
   e. In his Cross and Resurrection he justified us (CCC, no. 517).
4. Christ's whole earthly life—words, deeds, silences, sufferings—is a Revelation of the Father. Even the least characteristics of the mysteries of Jesus' life manifest God's love among us (CCC, no. 516).

III. Christ Our Light: Redemption Unfolds

A. The Baptism of Jesus and Jesus' triple temptation (CCC, nos. 538-540).
B. The miracle at the wedding feast of Cana (CCC, no. 2618).
C. The announcement of the Kingdom through parables and miracles (CCC, nos. 541-550).
D. Transfiguration at Mount Tabor (CCC, nos. 554-556).
E. Jesus institutes the Sacrament of the Eucharist (CCC, nos. 611, 1337-1344).

IV. Redemption Through the Paschal Mystery

A. The Passion and Death of Jesus (CCC, nos. 595-618).
1. The mystery of redemptive love and suffering on the cross.
   a. Overcoming temptation by Satan.
   b. Events of the Passion . . . the Suffering Servant.
   c. The Kenosis: Philippians 2:5-11.
B. The Resurrection of Jesus: redemption accomplished and the promise fulfilled (CCC, nos. 631-658).
1. A historical event involving Christ's physical body.
   a. Testified to by those who saw the Risen Jesus.
   b. Verified by the empty tomb.
2. A transcendent event in which Jesus is no longer bound by space and time.
   a. The Resurrection is not a resuscitation or a return to earthly life.
3. The significance of Christ's Resurrection.
   a. Confirmation of Jesus' divinity and of his words and teachings (CCC, nos. 651, 653).
   b. Fulfillment of the promises in the Old Testament and of Jesus' earthly promises (CCC, no. 652).
   c. A promise of our own resurrection (1 Cor 15).
4. We participate in the mystery of redemption through the sacramental life of the Church, especially the Holy Eucharist.
C. The Ascension and glorification of Jesus culminating in the sending of the Holy Spirit at Pentecost (CCC, nos. 659-667).
1. The Ascension marks the entrance of Jesus' humanity into heaven (CCC, no. 659).
2. Jesus' promise to be with us forever (Mt 28:20); the sending of the Holy Spirit as part of the promise.

3. Where Jesus has gone, we hope to follow; Mary, through her Assumption into heaven body and soul, is an anticipation of the resurrection of others who will follow (CCC, nos. 963-970).

V. Moral Implications for the Life of a Believer

A. Christ was put to death for our sins and was raised for our justification (Rom 4:25; CCC, no. 598).
   1. Eternal life with God in heaven is God's desire for us (CCC, nos. 1691-1698).
   2. We need to accept and live the grace of redemption (CCC, no. 1803).
      a. By practicing the virtues of faith, hope, and love (CCC, nos. 1812-1832).
      b. By praying for the coming of the Kingdom of God and by working toward that goal.
   3. Death and our judgment by God (CCC, nos. 678-679, 1006-1014).
      a. Immediate or particular judgment (CCC, no. 1021).
      b. The resurrection of the body and the Last Judgment (CCC, nos. 988-1004).
      c. Heaven, hell, purgatory (CCC, nos. 1023-1037).

B. Universal call to holiness of life (CCC, nos. 826, 2012-2014, 2028, 2045, 2813).
   1. We are made in the image of God: intellect and free will (CCC, nos. 1703-1706).
   2. Personal response to God's call is shown in our way of life (CCC, no. 2002).
   3. Holy Spirit and grace enable us to live holiness of life (CCC, no. 1704).
   4. Essential elements of a life growing in holiness: interiority or reflection, self-examination, and introspection (CCC, no. 1779).
   5. We grow in holiness of life in and through the Church (CCC, no. 2045).

C. Living as a disciple of Jesus.
   1. Adherence to Jesus and acceptance of his teaching (CCC, nos. 520, 618, 767, 1693).
   2. Conversion of heart and life, and the formation of conscience (CCC, no. 1248).
   3. Worshiping and loving God as Jesus taught (CCC, nos. 618, 767).
   4. Living a sacramental life and a life of prayer (CCC, nos. 562, 915, 1816, 1823, 1986, 2262, 2347, 2427, 2466, 2612).
   5. Putting Jesus' moral and spiritual teaching into practice.
   6. Serving the poor and marginalized.
   7. Fulfilling responsibility for the mission of evangelization.
   8. Fulfilling responsibility for stewardship.

VI. Prayer in the Life of a Believer

A. God calls every individual to a vital relationship with him experienced in prayer (CCC, no. 2558).

B. Developing intimacy and communion with Jesus Christ through prayer is an essential aspect in the life of a believer or disciple (CT, no. 5; GDC, no. 80; NDC, §19B; CCC, no. 2560).

C. Scripture is a source and guide for prayer (CCC, nos. 2567-2589, 2653-2654).
   1. Scripture is a source, in that many prayers come out of the Bible or are partly based on Scriptural passages or events: Mass prayers and dialogues, psalms and canticles, Our Father, Hail Mary, *Angelus* (CCC, nos. 2673-2679).
   2. Scripture is a guide, in that it gives us models of praying in biblical figures and teaches us about prayer.
   3. *Lectio divina* is a way of praying on the Word of God.

D. Expressions of prayer can be vocal, meditative, or contemplative (CCC, nos. 2700-2724).

E. The forms of prayer are blessing, adoration, petition, intercession, thanksgiving, and praise (CCC, nos. 2626-2649).

F. Prayer requires effort and commitment (CCC, nos. 2729-2745).

G. The Lord's Prayer forms a basis for the Church's understanding of the value of prayer (CCC, nos. 2759-2865).

VII. Challenges

A. Why would God the Father allow his Son, Jesus, to suffer and die the way he did (CCC, nos. 599-609)?
   1. God the Father allowed Jesus Christ, his Son, to suffer and die the way he did because of his love for all human beings; in that love, he wants us to live eternally with him in heaven. His Passion reveals the depth of the Father's love in helping all people to not be overcome by the magnitude of evil, sin, and death.

2. Because of Adam and Eve's sin, all human beings are born with a wounded human nature due to the absence of the life of Christ's grace, and so we could not live eternally with God unless we were redeemed (CCC, nos. 402-406).
3. God the Father allowed his Son, Jesus, to suffer and die because Jesus' sacrifice destroyed the power of sin and restored us to friendship with God.
4. In part, the Father allowed Jesus to suffer and die the way he did in order to show us the gravity and seriousness of sin.

B. Why are followers of Jesus Christ sometimes so willing to make sacrifices and to accept pain and suffering, especially in witness to Christ and their faith?
 1. Christians are willing to make sacrifices and undergo suffering patiently for a number of reasons.
    a. They are following the example of Jesus Christ, who through his suffering and Death gained salvation for us (CCC, no. 1505).
    b. Jesus Christ also predicted that people would suffer for their faith and promised that he would be with them in their suffering. Knowing this, believers try to accept suffering patiently, to trust in God, and to pray for his grace to sustain them. They rely on the Holy Spirit's gift of fortitude to grow in the virtue of fortitude (CCC, nos. 1808, 1831).
    c. Followers of Jesus Christ know that suffering is never in vain because it can help one move toward Heaven and eternal life. In our suffering, we can help make up to some degree for the hurt and harm we cause by our sin.
    d. Finally, the suffering, Death, Resurrection, and Ascension of Jesus teaches us to look beyond the sufferings of this world to the promise of eternal life with God in heaven (CCC, no. 1521).

 2. Christ strengthens the person to undergo suffering and thereby become more like Christ himself. Our suffering, when united with his own, can become a means of purification and of salvation for us and for others (CCC, nos. 618, 1505).

C. Isn't making sacrifices and putting up with suffering a sign of weakness (CCC, nos. 1808, 1831)?
 1. No. Making sacrifices and putting up with suffering requires a great deal of courage and strength. Jesus teaches us, by example, about the value of unselfish living and the courage and strength that requires. It takes grace and personal holiness to live as Jesus Christ has taught us.
 2. Jesus shows us through the whole Paschal Mystery (suffering, Death, Resurrection, and Ascension) that giving of ourselves is the path to eternal life and happiness (CCC, nos. 571-655).
 3. He gives us the example of accepting the Father's will even when it involves suffering.
 4. Jesus teaches us both in word and by example to refrain from revenge and to forgive those who hurt or sin against us (CCC, nos. 2842-2845).
 5. Suffering is necessary to develop our maturity in Christ and to love our neighbor as Christ loves him (Col 1:24; CCC, nos. 1808, 1831).

D. In the end, isn't it really only the final result that matters?
 1. No. Every moral choice that a person makes has an effect on the person and society (CCC, nos. 1749-1756).
 2. A good end never justifies an evil means (CCC, no. 1753).
 3. One must never do evil just so that good may come of it (CCC, no. 1789).

IV. Jesus Christ's Mission Continues in the Church

The purpose of this course is to help the students understand that in and through the Church they encounter the living Jesus Christ. They will be introduced to the fact that the Church was founded by Christ through the Apostles and is sustained by him through the Holy Spirit. The students will come to know that the Church is the living Body of Christ today. This Body has both divine and human elements. In this course, students will learn not so much about events in the life of the Church but about the sacred nature of the Church.

I. Christ Established His One Church to Continue His Presence and His Work

A. The origin, foundation, and manifestation of the Church (CCC, nos. 778-779).
 1. The Church—planned by the Father (LG, no. 2; CCC, no. 759).
 2. Preparation for the Church begins with God's promise to Abraham (CCC, no. 762).
 3. The Catholic Church was instituted by Christ (CCC, nos. 748-766).
    a. Christ inaugurated the Church by preaching Good News (CCC, nos. 767-768).
    b. Christ endowed his community with a structure that will remain until the Kingdom is fully achieved (CCC, no. 765).
    c. The Church is born primarily of Christ's total self-giving (CCC, no. 766).
 4. The Holy Spirit revealed the Church at Pentecost (CCC, nos. 767-768).
 5. Church is pillar and foundation of truth (1 Tm 3:15; CCC, no. 768).
B. The descent of the Holy Spirit (CCC, nos. 696, 731-732, 767, 1076, 1287, 2623).
 1. Fifty-day preparation.
 2. Jesus remains with us always.
 3. The events of the first Pentecost.
C. Holy Spirit is present in the entire Church (CCC, nos. 737-741).
 1. Spirit present in and through the Church.
 2. The Holy Spirit bestows varied hierarchic and charismatic gifts upon the Church.
 3. The Spirit's gifts help the Church to fulfill her mission (CCC, no. 768; LG, no. 4).
D. Holy Spirit inspires Apostles' mission (CCC, nos. 857, 860).
 1. The Great Commission (CCC, nos. 858-860).
 2. The preaching of Peter on Pentecost (CCC, nos. 551-556).
 3. The growth of the Church (CCC, nos. 766-769).
 4. Conflict with Jewish and Roman authorities (CCC, no. 2474).
    a. Persecutions (CCC, nos. 675-677, 769, 1816).
    b. Martyrdoms: Stephen, James (CCC, nos. 2473-2474).
 5. The Church spreads to the Gentiles (CCC, nos. 762, 774-776, 781).
    a. The conversion of St. Paul (CCC, no. 442).
    b. Paul's missionary journeys (CCC, no. 442).
E. Handing on the teaching of Jesus (CCC, nos. 787-789, 792, 796).
 1. Apostolic Tradition (CCC, nos. 857-865).
 2. The development of the New Testament (CCC, nos. 124-133).
F. The role of the Apostles in the early Church (CCC, no. 857).
 1. Chosen and appointed by Jesus Christ (CCC, nos. 857-860).
 2. The Council of Jerusalem: the Apostles recognized as leaders of the Church (CCC, no. 860).
 3. Community of Apostles continued in community of pope and bishops (CCC, nos. 861-862).

II. Images of the Church (Partial Insights of Church Sharing in Trinitarian Communion)

A. In the Old Testament (CCC, nos. 753-762).
 1. Prefigured in Noah's ark (CCC, nos. 56, 753, 845, 1219).
 2. The call of Abraham, and the promise to him of descendants (CCC, no. 762).
 3. Israel's election as the People of God (CCC, no. 762).
 4. The remnant foretold by the prophets (CCC, no. 762).
B. From the New Testament (CCC, nos. 763-776).
 1. The Body of Christ (CCC, nos. 787-795).
 2. The temple of the Holy Spirit (CCC, nos. 797-801).

3. The bride of Christ (CCC, no. 796).
   4. The vine and branches (CCC, no. 787).
   5. The seed and the beginning of the Kingdom (CCC, nos. 541, 669, 764, 768).
   6. The family of God (CCC, nos. 791, 1655-1658, 2204-2685).
C. Images rooted in Scripture and developed in Tradition.
   1. The People of God (CCC, nos. 781-782).
   2. The way to salvation.
   3. Marian images (CCC, nos. 507, 773, 967, 972).
   4. The community of disciples.
   5. A pilgrim people.

III. The Marks of the Church

"The sole Church of Christ which in the Creed we profess to be one, holy, catholic, and apostolic . . . subsists in the Catholic Church" (CCC, no. 870).

A. The Church is one (CCC, nos. 813-822).
   1. Unity is in Jesus Christ through the Holy Spirit; it is visible unity in the world.
   2. The Church is united in charity, in the profession of one faith, in the common celebration of worship and sacraments, and in Apostolic Succession (CCC, no. 815).
   3. Unity in diversity.
      a. Multiplicity of peoples, cultures, and liturgical traditions (CCC, nos. 814, 1202).
      b. Communion of twenty-one Eastern Catholic Churches and one Western Church, all in union with the Pope.
   4. Wounds to unity.
      a. Heresies (note modern parallels).
         1) Early Church heresies: Gnosticism, Arianism, Nestorianism, Monophysitism, and Apollinarianism (CCC, nos. 464, 466-467, 471).
         2) Protestant Reformation: emphasized *sola scriptura* (the Bible alone) and *sola gratia* (grace alone).
         3) New divisions—sects and cults.
      b. Schisms (the split between East and West).
         1) Following the Council of Ephesus in 431, those Churches which followed Nestorius established separate Churches; later returned to union with Rome.
         2) Following the Council of Chalcedon in 451, those who accepted the Monophysite position formed what are called the Oriental Orthodox Churches.
         3) Eastern Schism of 1054: the pope in Rome and the bishop of Constantinople excommunicated each other, thus leading to the breach between the Roman Catholic Church and the Eastern Orthodox Church.
      c. Apostasy.
   5. Ecumenism.
      a. Jesus' prayer for unity of his disciples (Jn 17:11; CCC, no. 820).
      b. Vatican II documents.
      c. Ecumenical dialogues with Orthodox Churches and Protestant ecclesial and faith communities emphasized common baptism of all Christians and common service to love even to the point of joint-martyrdom.
      d. The fullness of Christ's Church subsists in the Catholic Church (LG, no. 8).
   6. Interreligious Dialogue.
      a. Judaism, which holds a unique place in relation to the Catholic Church.
      b. Islam.
      c. Other religions.

B. The Church is holy (CCC, nos. 823-829).
   1. Holiness is from the all-holy God: all human beings are called to live in holiness.
   2. Christ sanctifies the Church through the Holy Spirit and grants the means of holiness to the Church.
   3. Church members must cooperate with God's grace.
      a. Divine dimensions of the Church.
      b. Human dimensions of the Church.
   4. Church members sin, but the Church as Body of Christ is sinless.
      a. Church constantly fosters conversion and renewal.
   5. Mary, Mother of the Church and model of faith.
      a. The Annunciation and Mary's "yes" to God.
      b. Mary's perpetual virginity.
      c. The Immaculate Conception and the Assumption.
   6. Canonized saints: models of holiness.
      a. Their example encourages us.
      b. They intercede for us.

7. The members of the Church are always in need of purification, penance, and renewal (LG, no. 8, cited in CCC, nos. 827, 1428; UR, no. 6, cited in CCC, no. 821).
C. The Church is catholic (CCC, nos. 830-856).
   1. The Church has been sent by Christ on a mission to the whole world and exists worldwide.
   2. The Church exists for all people and is the means to salvation for all people.
   3. Salvation comes from the Church even for non-members (see *Dominus Iesus*, section 20; CCC, no. 1257).
D. The Church is apostolic (CCC, nos. 857-865).
   1. Founded by Christ on the Twelve with the primacy of Peter.
   2. Has apostolic mission and teaching of Scripture and Tradition.
   3. Guided by successors of the Twelve: the pope and bishops.
   4. Christ calls all Church members to share Gospel of salvation.

IV. The Church in the World

A. The Church is sign and instrument of communion with God and unity of the human race (CCC, no. 760).
B. Christ founded the Church with a divine purpose and mission (CCC, no. 760).
   1. Jesus—not the members—endowed Church with authority, power, and responsibility (CCC, nos. 763-766).
   2. Church transcends history yet is part of history.
   3. Church continues Christ's salvation, preserves and hands on his teaching.
   4. Church scrutinizes "signs of the times"—interprets them in light of Gospel.
C. The Church and her mission of evangelization (CCC, nos. 861, 905).
   1. Definition and description of evangelization.
   2. Missionary efforts.
   3. Call to a new evangelization.
D. Visible structure of the Church: a hierarchical communion (CCC, nos. 880-896).
   1. The College of Bishops in union with the pope as its head.
      a. The Holy See.
      b. Individual dioceses.
      c. Parishes.
      d. Family: the domestic Church (CCC, nos. 791, 1655-1658, 2204, 2685).
   2. The various vocations of life.
      a. Ordained bishops, diocesan and religious priests continue the ministry of Christ the Head (CCC, nos. 1555-1568).
      b. Ordained deacons continue the ministry of Christ the Servant (CCC, nos. 1569-1571).
      c. Religious: consecrated by vows to Christ (CCC, nos. 925-933).
         1) Religious orders.
         2) Religious societies.
      d. Laity: baptized members of Christ (CCC, nos. 897-913).
         1) Evangelization and sanctification of the world.
         2) Some of the laity work full time for the Church.
         3) The laity live in various states of life:
            a) Marriage and family life.
            b) Single life.
            c) Third orders and lay consecrated people.
E. Teaching office in the Church: the Magisterium (CCC, no. 890).
   1. The teaching role of the pope and bishops.
      a. Authentic interpreters of God's Word in Scripture and Tradition.
      b. Ensure fidelity to teachings of the Apostles on faith and morals (CCC, Glossary).
      c. Explain the hierarchy of truths.
      d. The Ordinary Magisterium must be accepted even when it is not pronounced in a definitive manner.
      e. Obey the mandate for evangelization.
   2. Indefectibility and infallibility.
      a. Indefectibility: the Church will always teach the Gospel of Christ without error even in spite of the defects of her members, both ordained and lay.
      b. Infallibility: the gift of the Holy Spirit, which gives the Church the ability to teach faith and morals without error.
         1) The pope can exercise infallibility when teaching alone on faith and morals, when the teaching is held in common by the bishops of the world and the pope declares that he is teaching *ex cathedra* (CCC, no. 891).

                2) The pope and bishops exercise infallibility when they teach together either in regular teaching dispersed throughout the world or when gathered in an ecumenical council (CCC, no. 892).
         3. The law of the Church.
              a. Pastoral norms for living the faith and moral life, e.g., the precepts of the Church.
              b. Disciplines of the Church can be adjusted by the hierarchy for new circumstances.
    F. Sanctifying office of the Church (CCC, no. 893).
         1. The Eucharist is the center of life in the Church.
         2. Bishops and priests sanctify the Church by prayer, work and ministry of the Word, and the sacraments.
         3. Goal for all is eternal life.
    G. Governing office of the Church (CCC, nos. 894-896).
         1. The pope, the bishop of Rome, exercises supreme, ordinary, and immediate jurisdiction over the universal Church.
         2. Bishops have responsibility to govern their particular churches; they are to exercise their authority and sacred power with the Good Shepherd as their model.

V. Implications for Life of a Believer

A. Belonging to the Church is essential (CCC, no. 760).
    1. Christ willed the Church to be the ordinary way and means of salvation (CCC, no. 763, 772-776).
    2. We receive Christ's redemption as members of his Body the Church.
    3. Christ entrusted Word and sacraments to the Church for our salvation.
    4. Church has fullness of truth and totality of the means of salvation.
B. Jesus Christ enriches us through the Church.
    1. Through the sacraments beginning with Baptism; regular reception of the sacraments is essential for members of the Church.
    2. Through a life of prayer, communion, charity, service, and justice in the household of faith.
    3. Through association with others who want to follow Christ in the Church.
C. The Church at prayer.
    1. Liturgical year (CCC, nos. 1163-1178).
    2. How we pray.
    3. Celebration of the Christian mysteries (CCC, nos. 1273, 1389).
D. Living as a member of the Church, the Body of Christ, means we live as disciples, proclaiming the Lord Jesus' teaching to others (CCC, nos. 520, 1248).
    1. As disciples of Christ we are "salt and light for the world."
         a. Living as Christ calls and teaches us as known in and through the Church.
         b. Active response to call to holiness at home, workplace, public square.
         c. Examples for Christian witness in parish and diocese.
    2. Necessity of prayer (CCC, nos. 2612, 2621).
         a. The Lord forms, teaches, guides, consoles, and blesses us through prayer.
         b. Prayer helps us understand the teachings of Jesus Christ and his Church in a deeper way and live them more fully.

VI. Challenges

A. Why do I have to be a Catholic? Aren't all religions as good as another (CCC, nos. 760, 817-822, 836)?
    1. To be a Catholic is to be a member of the one true Church of Christ. While elements of truth can be found in other churches and religions, the fullness of the means of salvation subsists in the Catholic Church (CCC, nos. 816, 836-838).
    2. Christ willed that the Catholic Church be his sacrament of salvation, the sign and the instrument of the communion of God and man (CCC, nos. 774-776, 780).
    3. Christ established his Church as a visible organization through which he communicates his grace, truth, and salvation (CCC, no. 771).
    4. Those who through no fault of their own do not know Christ or the Catholic Church are not excluded from salvation; in a way known to God, all people are offered the possibility of salvation through the Church (CCC, nos. 836-848).
    5. Members of the Catholic Church have the duty to evangelize others (CCC, nos. 849-856).
B. Isn't the Church being hypocritical in telling other people to be holy and avoid sin when many Catholics, including the clergy, are guilty of terrible wrongs (CCC, nos. 823-829)?
    1. Some members of the Church might be hypocritical. Members of the Church, like all human beings, are guilty of sin, but this doesn't make the Church wrong or hypocritical.

2. The Church teaches what God has told us about how to be holy and the necessity of avoiding sin. Failure by members of the Church to live out what God has taught does not invalidate the truth of the teaching we have received through the Apostles and their successors.
3. The Church is guided and animated by the Holy Spirit and, as the Body of Christ, remains sinless even if her members sin.

C. Who needs organized religion? Isn't it better to worship God in my own way, when and how I want?
1. God desires us to come to him as members of his family, his new people, so he established the Church to accomplish that purpose (CCC, no. 760).
2. No one and no community can proclaim the Gospel to themselves (CCC, no. 875).
3. Because human beings are social in nature, we need each other's encouragement, support, and example (CCC, no. 820).
4. Worship of God has both a personal dimension and a communal dimension: personal, private worship is encouraged to complement communal worship (CCC, nos. 821, 1136-1144).
5. The Church offers us authentic worship in spirit and in truth when we unite ourselves with Christ's self-offering in the Mass (CCC, nos. 1322-1324).
6. God taught in the Old and New Testaments for people to come together and worship in the way that he revealed to them (CCC, nos. 1093-1097).
7. The Catholic Church is structured so that all the members, clergy and laity alike, are accountable to someone (CCC, nos. 871-879).

D. How is it that the Catholic Church is able to sustain the unity of her members even though they live out their faith in different cultures and sometimes express their faith in different ways?
1. The Church is able to sustain unity because she has the apostolic teaching office of the pope and bishops to guide and direct her under the guidance of the Holy Spirit (CCC, no. 815).
2. It is the pope and bishops who are the successors in every age to St. Peter and the Apostles (CCC, nos. 815, 862).
3. The unity of the Church is also sustained through the common celebration of worship and the sacraments (CCC, no. 815).

V. Sacraments as Privileged Encounters with Jesus Christ

The purpose of this course is to help students understand that they can encounter Christ today in a full and real way in and through the sacraments, and especially through the Eucharist. Students will examine each of the sacraments in detail so as to learn how they may encounter Christ throughout life.

I. The Sacramental Nature of the Church

A. Definition of sacrament.
   1. A sacrament is an efficacious sign of grace, instituted by Christ and entrusted to the Church, by which divine life of grace is dispensed to us through the work of the Holy Spirit (CCC, no. 1131).
   2. Eastern Churches use the word "mystery" for sacrament and celebrate them in a similar but not essentially different way.
   3. Sacraments confer the grace they signify (CCC, no. 1127).
      a. Grace: sanctifying and actual—gratuitous (CCC, nos. 1996-2005).
      b. Sacramental grace (CCC, no. 1129).
B. The Church and the sacramental economy of salvation (CCC, no. 849).
   1. Jesus Christ is the living, ever-present sacrament of God (CCC, nos. 1088-1090).
   2. The Church as universal sacrament of Jesus Christ (CCC, nos. 774-776).
      a. The Church is the sacrament of salvation, the sign and the instrument of the communion of God and all (CCC, no. 780).
      b. The Church has a sacramental view of all reality (CCC, no. 739).
      c. The Church is the sacrament of the Trinity's communion with us (CCC, no. 774).
C. Redemption is mediated through the seven sacraments.
   1. Christ acts through the sacraments (CCC, nos. 1084-1085).
      a. Signs and symbols (CCC, nos. 1145-1152).
      b. Sacraments for healing and sanctification (CCC, nos. 1123, 1421).
      c. Experiential sign of Christ's presence (CCC, nos. 1115-1116).
   2. The Church at prayer (CCC, no. 1073).
      a. Prayer defined; different forms (CCC, nos. 2559, 2565).
      b. Essential for a believer (CCC, no. 2558).
      c. Liturgical prayer and the sacraments (CCC, nos. 1137-1144).
      d. Personal prayer; Christian meditation (CCC, nos. 2626-2643, 2705-2719).

II. The Sacraments of Initiation (CCC, no. 1212)

A. Baptism: the sacrament which is the birth of the baptized into new life in Christ. In Baptism, Original Sin is forgiven along with all personal sins. By it we become adoptive children of the Father, members of Christ, and temples of the Holy Spirit; it also incorporates us into the Church and makes us sharers in the priesthood of Christ (CCC, nos. 1279-1280).
   1. Understanding the sacrament.
      a. Scriptural basis.
         1) The Sacrament of Baptism is pre-figured in the Old Testament at creation when the Spirit of God hovered over the waters at creation (Gn 1–2); in Noah's ark (Gn 7); in the crossing of the Red Sea (Ex 14) and the Jordan (CCC, nos. 1217-1222).
         2) New Testament references: Mt 3:1-12; Mt 3:13-17; Mt 29:19; Mk 1:9-11; Lk 3:21-22; Jn 1:22-34; Jn 3:1-15; Acts 2:37-41 (CCC, nos. 1223-1225).
      b. Historical development (CCC, nos. 1229-1233).
         1) Baptism of blood (CCC, no. 1258).
         2) Baptism of desire (CCC, nos. 1258-1261).
      c. Theology (CCC, nos. 1217-1228).
   2. Celebration (CCC, nos. 1229-1245).
      a. Baptism of adults (CCC, nos. 1247-1249).
      b. Baptism of infants (CCC, nos. 403, 1231, 1233, 1250-1252, 1282, 1290).
         1) The question of infants who die before Baptism (CCC, no. 1283).
      c. Role of godparents (CCC, no. 1255).
   3. Essential elements (CCC, nos. 1239-1240).
      a. Immersion or the triple pouring of water on the head (CCC, nos. 694, 1214, 1217, 1240).

b. Saying the words of the formula (CCC, no. 1240).
4. Other elements: (CCC, nos. 1237-1245).
5. Effects of the sacrament (CCC, nos. 1262-1270).
   a. Die and rise with Christ (CCC, no. 1227).
   b. Freed from Original Sin and all sins (CCC, no. 1263).
   c. Adopted children of God (CCC, nos. 1265-1266).
   d. Members of the Church (CCC, nos. 1267-1270).
   e. Indelible character; this sacrament cannot be repeated (CCC, nos. 1272-1274).
   f. Holy Spirit and discipleship (CCC, no. 1241).
6. Requirements for reception.
   a. For adults (CCC, nos. 1247-1249).
   b. For infants (CCC, nos. 1250-1252).
   c. Catechesis for baptized (CCC, nos. 1253-1255).
7. Minister of the sacrament (CCC, no. 1256).
   a. Ordinary circumstances.
   b. In danger of death.
8. Necessity of Baptism (CCC, nos. 1257-1261).
9. Implications.
   a. Members of Church (CCC, no. 1267).
   b. Common priesthood (CCC, no. 1268).
   c. Rights and duties (CCC, no. 1269).
   d. Call to mission (CCC, no. 1270).
   e. Ecumenical aspect (CCC, no. 1271).
10. Appropriating and living this sacrament (CCC, no. 1694).
    a. Reminders of our Baptism.
       1) In the Church's liturgy: Easter vigil, renewal of baptismal promises, sprinkling rite at Mass (CCC, nos. 281, 1217, 1254, 1668, 2719).
       2) In pious practices: blessing with holy water (fonts in churches and homes), sign of the cross (CCC, no. 1668).
    b. Prayer and reflection on the meaning of Baptism (CCC, nos. 1694, 1811, 1966, 1988, 1987, 1992, 1997, 2015).
       1) Sharing in the Death and Resurrection of Christ.
       2) Turning away from sin and selfish actions; ongoing conversion.

B. Confirmation: the sacrament in which the gift of the Holy Spirit received at Baptism is confirmed, strengthened, and perfected for living the Christian life and spreading the faith to others; in this sacrament we receive a permanent sign or character so it cannot be repeated.
   1. Understanding the sacrament.
      a. Scriptural basis.
         1) The book of Isaiah foretold that the Spirit of the Lord shall rest on the hoped-for Messiah (Is 11:2; CCC, no. 1286).
         2) The Holy Spirit descended on the Church (Acts 8:14-17; CCC, nos. 1287-1288).
      b. Historical development (CCC, nos. 1290-1292).
      c. Theology.
         1) Western Church (CCC, nos. 1286-1288).
         2) Eastern Churches (CCC, no. 1289).
   2. Celebration.
      a. Rite of Confirmation (CCC, nos. 1298-1300).
      b. Rite of Christian Initiation of Adults (RCIA) (CCC, nos. 1232-1233, 1298).
      c. Eastern Catholic Churches confirm (chrismate) at the time of Baptism and, in some cases, administer Eucharist then as well (CCC, nos. 1290-1292).
   3. Essential elements of the sacrament (CCC, no. 1300).
      a. Laying-on of hands and anointing with chrism.
      b. Saying the words of the formula.
   4. Requirements for reception.
      a. Baptized and age (CCC, nos. 1306-1308).
      b. Preparation, Confession, sponsor (CCC, nos. 1309-1310).
   5. Minister (CCC, nos. 1312-1314).
   6. Effects and implications (CCC, no. 1303).
      a. Perfection of baptismal grace (CCC, no. 1285).
      b. Help of Holy Spirit's gifts and fruits (CCC, nos. 1830-1832).
      c. Indelible character; this sacrament cannot be repeated (CCC, nos. 1303-1305).
      d. Call to spread and defend faith (CCC, no. 1303).
      e. Discernment of God's call (CCC, no. 1303).
      f. Stewardship (CCC, no. 1303).
   7. Appropriating and living this sacrament: life in the Holy Spirit (CCC, no. 1694).

a. How to know the Holy Spirit's promptings and actions in your life, with the help of the Holy Spirit (CCC, no. 1694).
    1) Learn Sacred Scripture (CCC, nos. 50-51, 94-95, 1066).
    2) Live the sacraments (CCC, nos. 1071-1072, 1091-1092).
    3) Love the Catholic Church—the Church that Christ began.
b. Prayer is the foundation for knowing and following the will and actions of the Holy Spirit (CCC, nos. 1309, 1073, 2670-2672).

C. Holy Eucharist: the sacrament which re-presents in the Mass the sacrificial Death of Christ and his Resurrection—making it possible for us to eat his Body and drink his Blood (CCC, no. 1323).
  1. Understanding the sacrament.
      a. Scriptural basis: Ex 12; Mt 14:13-21; Mt 26: 26-29; Mk 6:30-33; Mk 14:22-25; Lk 9:10-17; Lk 22:14-20; Jn 2:1-12; Jn 6:22-59; Jn 13–17; 1 Cor 11:23ff. (CCC, nos. 1337-1344).
          1) The Eucharist is pre-figured in the Old Testament, beginning with the priest-king Melchizedek (Gn 14:18-20), Israel eating unleavened bread every year at Passover, and Yahweh providing manna from heaven (CCC, nos. 1333, 1544).
      b. Historical development (CCC, nos. 1324-1332, 1345).
      c. Theology.
          1) Signs (CCC, nos. 1333-1336).
          2) Institution (CCC, nos. 1337-1340).
          3) "In memory" (CCC, nos. 1341-1343).
          4) Thanksgiving and praise (CCC, nos. 1359-1361).
          5) Sacrificial memorial (CCC, nos. 1362-1372).
          6) *Ecclesia de Eucharistia.*
  2. Celebration.
      a. Parts of the Mass (CCC, nos. 1348-1355).
      b. Roles of priests and deacons (CCC, nos. 1566, 1570).
      c. Roles of faith community (CCC, nos. 1140, 1348).
  3. Essential elements.
      a. Bread (unleavened in Latin Church, leavened in Eastern Churches) and wine from grapes (CCC, no. 1412; CIC, cc. 924 §§1-3, 926, 927).
      b. Eucharistic Prayer (CCC, nos. 1352-1355).
  4. Christ's Real Presence.
      a. Transubstantiation (CCC, nos. 1373-1377).
      b. Worship of the Eucharist.
          1) Adoration (CCC, no. 1378).
          2) Tabernacle (CCC, no. 1379).
          3) Reverence (CCC, nos. 1385-1386, 1418).
  5. Effects of the sacrament.
      a. Union with Jesus and Church (CCC, nos. 1391, 1396).
      b. Forgiveness of venial sin (CCC, no. 1394).
      c. Protection from grave sin (CCC, no. 1395).
      d. Commits us to the poor (CCC, no. 1397).
  6. Requirements for fruitful reception.
      a. Baptized member of the Church who believes in the Real Presence and Transubstantiation (CCC, nos. 1376, 1385, 1387-1388).
      b. Free from grave sin (CCC, no. 1385).
      c. One hour fast from food and drink (CCC, no. 1387).
  7. Other receptions.
      a. Frequent Communion (CCC, nos. 1388-1389).
      b. Viaticum (CCC, nos. 1524-1525).
      c. Eucharist two times a day (CIC, c. 917).
  8. Minister of the sacrament (CCC, nos. 1369, 1566).
  9. Role of extraordinary ministers of Holy Communion (CCC, no. 1411; CIC, c. 910 §2, c. 230 §3).
  10. Implications.
      a. Ecumenical (CCC, no. 1398).
      b. Love of God, neighbor, and poor (CCC, nos. 1396-1397).
      c. Nourishing Christ's life in us (CCC, no. 1392).
  11. Appropriating and living this sacrament.
      a. Active participation in Mass where the Lord comes in both word and sacrament (CCC, nos. 2042, 2181-2182).
      b. Prayer of thanksgiving on receiving Jesus Christ in the Eucharist (CCC, nos. 1358-1359).
      c. Reflective prayer on the meaning of Christ's Death and Resurrection, and petition for the grace to give to others of ourselves as the Lord did (CCC, nos. 1359-1361).

III. Sacraments of Healing

A. Penance and Reconciliation: the sacrament through which sins committed after Baptism can be forgiven, and reconciliation with God and community can be effected (CCC, nos. 1422, 1425, 1428, 1446).

1. Understanding the sacrament.
    a. Scriptural basis: Jesus gives the Eleven the power to forgive sins (Jn 20:22-23). Examples of forgiveness (Mk 2:1-12; Lk 15:11-32; Jn 8:1-11; CCC, no. 1444).
    b. Historical development (CCC, nos. 1425-1429, 1447-1448).
    c. Theology (CCC, nos. 1440-1449).
2. Celebration.
    a. Individual confession (CCC, nos. 1456-1458, 1480, 1484).
    b. Communal service (CCC, no. 1482).
    c. General absolution (CCC, no. 1483).
3. Essential elements.
    a. Acts of the penitent: contrition and firm purpose of amendment, confession of sins, penance or satisfaction (CCC, nos. 1450-1458).
    b. Absolution (CCC, nos. 1480-1484).
4. Effects.
    a. Forgiveness of all sin (CCC, no. 1442).
    b. Reconciliation with God by which grace is received (CCC, nos. 1468-1469, 1496).
    c. Reconciliation with the Church (CCC, nos. 1443-1445).
    d. Remission of punishment for sin (CCC, nos. 1470, 1496).
    e. Peace and serenity (CCC, no. 1496).
    f. Spiritual strength to resist temptation (CCC, no. 1496).
5. Requirements for reception.
    a. Contrition, both perfect and imperfect (CCC, nos. 1451-1454).
    b. Confession of grave or mortal sins (CCC, nos. 1455-1457).
    c. Confession of venial sins recommended (CCC, no. 1458).
6. Minister of the sacrament (CCC, nos. 1461-1466).
    a. The seal of confession (CCC, no. 1467).
7. Implications (CCC, nos. 1468-1470).
    a. Thanksgiving and amendment (CCC, nos. 1459, 1451).
    b. Ongoing conversion (CCC, no. 1423).
    c. Reconciliation with the Church community (CCC, nos. 1422, 1443-1445, 1469).
8. Appropriating and living this sacrament (CCC, nos. 1451, 1468-1469, 1470).
    a. Prayer of thanksgiving for the gift of God's forgiveness of sins.
    b. Reflective prayer on contrition in its fullest sense: sorrow for our sins with the resolution to avoid future sin (CCC, no. 1452).

B. Anointing of the Sick: the sacrament which gives spiritual healing and strength to a person seriously ill and sometimes also physical recovery (CCC, nos. 1499-1513).
1. Understanding the sacrament.
    a. Scriptural basis: Jas 5:14-15 (CCC, no. 1510).
    b. Historical development (CCC, no. 1512).
    c. Theology.
        1) Illness (CCC, nos. 1500-1502).
        2) Christ the Physician (CCC, no. 1503).
        3) Faith and healing (CCC, no. 1504).
        4) Christ's suffering (CCC, no. 1505).
        5) Disciples carry cross (CCC, no. 1506).
        6) Holy Spirit's gift of healing (CCC, no. 1509).
        7) Christ institutes sacrament of the sick (CCC, nos. 1500-1513).
2. Celebration.
    a. Individual celebration (CCC, nos. 1514-1516).
    b. Communal celebration (CCC, nos. 1517-1518).
    c. Viaticum (CCC, nos. 1524-1525).
3. Essential elements (CCC, nos. 1517-1519).
    a. Laying-on of hands; anointing forehead and hands with oil of the sick.
    b. Spoken words of the formula.
4. Effects (CCC, nos. 1520-1523).
    a. Union of the sick person to Christ in his Passion.
    b. Strength, peace, and courage to endure the sufferings of illness or old age.
    c. The forgiveness of sins.
    d. The restoration of health if God wills it.
    e. Preparation for passing over to eternal life.
5. Requirements for reception (CCC, nos. 1514-1515).
6. Minister: priest or bishop (CCC, no. 1516).
7. Implications (CCC, no. 1532).
    a. The Lord Jesus does not abandon or forget us; he is with us in all things.
    b. The Lord Jesus' healing power is still at work in the world.
8. Appropriating and living this sacrament (CCC, nos. 1522-1523).
    a. Prayerful reflection on the healing power of Jesus Christ.
    b. Prayer on accepting God's will.
    c. Prayer on offering up our sufferings to God.

IV. Sacraments at the Service of Communion

A. Holy Orders: the sacrament through which a man is made a bishop, priest, or deacon and is given the grace and power to fulfill the responsibilities of the order to which he is ordained.
   1. Understanding the sacrament.
      a. Scriptural basis: Mt 16:18ff.; Mt 28:19-20; Lk 6:12-16; Mk 3:14-19 (CCC, no. 1577).
         1) Jesus consecrates his followers at the Last Supper (Jn 17).
         2) To remember him, Jesus commanded his followers, "Do this in memory of me." His Apostles continued to celebrate the Eucharist as ordained ministers.
      b. Historical development—instituted by Christ (CCC, nos. 874ff.).
      c. Theology (CCC, nos. 1539-1553).
   2. Celebration of Ordination.
      a. Bishop (CCC, nos. 1555-1561).
      b. Priest (CCC, nos. 1562-1568).
      c. Deacon (CCC, nos. 1569-1571).
   3. Essential elements (CCC, nos. 1572-1574).
      a. Imposition of hands.
      b. Spoken prayer of consecration.
   4. Effects.
      a. Indelible character; this sacrament cannot be repeated (CCC, nos. 1581-1584).
      b. Grace of the Holy Spirit (CCC, nos. 1585-1589).
   5. Requirements for reception.
      a. Called to ministry (CCC, no. 1578).
      b. Baptized male (CCC, no. 1577).
      c. Celibacy in the Latin Church (CCC, no. 1579).
      d. Adequate education and formation (CCC, nos. 1578, 1598).
      e. Mental health screening (*Program of Priestly Formation*, nos. 5, 53).
      f. Lifelong commitment to personal prayer and devotion (CCC, nos. 1567, 1579).
      g. Servant leader in Person of Christ (CCC, nos. 1552-1553, 1548-1551).
   6. Minister of the sacrament: bishop (CCC, nos. 1575-1576).
   7. Implications.
      a. Servant leaders according to order (CCC, nos. 1547ff.).
      b. Distinctive ministries of bishop, priest, and deacon (CCC, nos. 1594-1596).
   8. Appropriating and living this sacrament.
      a. Prayer for more vocations to the priesthood (CCC, no. 1548).
      b. Praying for bishops, priests, and deacons (CCC, no. 1547).
      c. Offering help and support to bishops, priests, and deacons (CCC, no. 1547).

B. Marriage: the sacrament in which a baptized man and a baptized woman form with each other a lifelong covenantal communion of life and love that signifies the union of Christ and the Church and through which they are given the grace to live out this union (CCC, nos. 1601, 1603, 1613-1616, 1642).
   1. Understanding the sacrament: Jesus raises marriage to the dignity of a sacrament.
      a. Scriptural basis: Jn 2:1-11; Mt 19:1-15; Mt 5:31-32 (CCC, nos. 1614-1615).
      b. Historical development (CCC, nos. 1602-1620).
      c. Theology.
         1) Sacramental marriage (CCC, nos. 1621-1630).
         2) Mixed marriages/disparity of cult (CCC, nos. 1633-1637).
            a) Conditions for permission/dispensation.
   2. Celebration.
      a. Within Mass (CCC, nos. 1621-1624).
      b. Within Liturgy of the Word.
   3. Essential elements.
      a. Free consent of the couple (CCC, nos. 1625-1629, 1632).
      b. Consent given in the presence of the Church's minister and two witnesses (CCC, nos. 1630-1631).
   4. Effects (CCC, nos. 1638-1642).
      a. Grace to perfect the couple's love for each other and strengthen their bond.
      b. Help to live the responsibilities of married life.
      c. Help on the journey to eternal life.
   5. Requirements for reception.
      a. Baptism (CCC, nos. 1617, 1625, 1633).
      b. No prior bond or other impediments (CCC, no. 1625).
      c. Able to give free consent (CCC, nos. 1625, 1627).
      d. Celebration of marriage according to Church law (CCC, nos. 1625-1637).
   6. Ministers: the spouses before priest or deacon and two other witnesses (CCC, nos. 1623, 1630).

(N.B. In Eastern Churches, the priest is the minister of the sacrament.)
7. The requirements of marriage.
   a. Unity and indissolubility (CCC, nos. 1644-1645).
   b. Fidelity (CCC, nos. 1646-51).
   c. Openness to children (CCC, nos. 1652-1654).
8. Divorce, declaration of nullity, remarriages (CCC, no. 1650).
9. Implications.
   a. Lifelong, conjugal fidelity (CCC, nos. 1646ff.).
   b. Domestic Church (CCC, nos. 1655-1658).
   c. Gift of children and nurturing them (CCC, nos. 1652-1653).
   d. Qualities of successful marriages (CCC, nos. 1641-1658).
10. Appropriating and living this sacrament.
    a. Prayer for parents, relatives, and all who are married (CCC, no. 1657).
    b. Praying for our lives ahead, asking God to help us know his will and to follow it in faith (CCC, no. 1656).
    c. Careful preparation for marriage, remote, proximate, and immediate (FC, no. 66; CCC, no. 1632).
    d. Ongoing marriage enrichment (CCC, nos. 1632, 1648).
    e. Reflective prayer on married life as witness to Christ's love (CCC, no. 1661).

V. Challenges to Worship and Sacraments

A. Can't a person go directly to God without the help of the Church or a priest (CCC, nos. 1538-1539)?
   1. Any person can always pray directly to God. However, God established the Church as a way for him to teach us and to enrich us with his grace. Jesus Christ gave us the Church and the sacraments for our salvation (CCC, nos. 774-776).
   2. Sacraments provide an encounter with Christ which is unique and graced (CCC, no. 1076).
   3. Sacraments celebrate and strengthen our unity and identity (CCC, no. 774).
B. Can't God forgive us directly when we are sorry for sin (CCC, nos. 1434, 1440-1445)?
   1. While God can forgive us however and whenever he wants, he knows what is best for us and has taught us through Jesus that he wants to forgive us through the Sacrament of Penance and Reconciliation (Jn 20:21-23; CCC, nos. 1421, 1442).
   2. The Sacrament of Reconciliation is necessary to forgive grave or mortal sins (CCC, no. 1468), but it is not essential for the forgiveness of venial sins (CCC, no. 1493).
   3. People need to confess sins to face the reality of the wrong they have done, and in and through this sacrament, they can be assured of forgiveness (CCC, nos. 1455-1457).
   4. The sacrament also gives the assurance of forgiveness to a truly repentant person (CCC, nos. 1452-1453).
C. Aren't the sacraments just celebrations to mark significant moments in our life (CCC, nos. 1066, 1070)?
   1. While the sacraments are usually celebrated at appropriate or significant moments or events in our lives, they are much more than simply celebrations of those moments. They are personal encounters with Christ, who acts through sacraments to help us (CCC, nos. 1088-1090).
   2. Each sacrament gives a special grace (CCC, no. 1129).
D. Is there any difference between receiving Holy Communion in a Catholic Church and going to communion in a Protestant worship service (CCC, no. 1411)?
   1. Yes, there are differences.
      a. Because of Apostolic Succession and the priesthood, Holy Eucharist in the Catholic Church is the Body and Blood of Jesus Christ. Churches without Apostolic Succession and the priesthood do not have that gift (CCC, nos. 817-822, 1411).
      b. Reception of Holy Communion in the Catholic Church is a statement of belief in the Real Presence of Jesus in the Eucharist and of unity with all Catholics throughout the world (CCC, nos. 1376, 1391, 1398).
   2. Because of these differences, Catholics must not take communion in Protestant worship services, and non-Catholics must not receive Holy Communion in Catholic Churches (CCC, no. 1411).
E. How do we know that any of the sacraments really work? For example, if a person dies after receiving the Sacrament of the Anointing of the Sick, does that mean it did not work (CCC, nos. 1500-1501, 1503-1505, 1508-1509, 1520-1523)?
   1. The effects of the grace we receive through the sacraments is not something that can be seen or measured.

2. Each of the sacraments is effective whether we feel it or not; it is sometimes only in looking back that we can recognize how Christ has touched us and helped us through the sacraments.

3. The Sacrament of the Anointing of the Sick can have different effects. Sometimes Christ does bring about physical healing through that sacrament. Other times, the healing is spiritual in that it helps the person to be better prepared for death, to be at peace, and to be eager to be with the Lord.

VI. Life in Jesus Christ

The purpose of this course is to help students understand that it is only through Christ that they can fully live out God's plans for their lives. Students are to learn the moral concepts and precepts that govern the lives of Christ's disciples.

I. What Is Life in Christ?

A. God's plan for us (CCC, nos. 302-314, 1692).
  1. God creates us to share eternal love and happiness with him in Heaven.
     a. Desire and longing for God (CCC, no. 27).
     b. Fall and promise of redemption (CCC, no. 410).
     c. Jesus Christ fulfills this promise (CCC, nos. 456-460).
  2. God created us in his image and likeness (CCC, nos. 1700-1706).
     a. The dignity of the human person (CCC, no. 1700).
     b. Endowed with reason, intellect, and free will (CCC, nos. 1703-1706).
B. Our response to God's plan.
  1. Response of love (CCC, no. 1828).
  2. He calls us to beatitude or joy.
     a. The Beatitudes (CCC, no. 1716).
     b. Effects of the Beatitudes (CCC, nos. 1718-1724).
     c. God's gift of joy (CCC, no. 1720).
  3. What it means to be a follower of Christ.
     a. Baptism and divine filiation (CCC, no. 1279).
     b. Focused on Christ (CCC, no. 1698).
     c. Moral life and happiness (CCC, nos. 1988ff.).

II. God Has Taught Us How to Live a New Life in Christ

A. God rules the universe with wisdom and directs its divine fulfillment (CCC, no. 1719).
  1. Eternal law (CCC, nos. 1950-1951).
  2. Divine Providence (CCC, no. 1975).
  3. Natural moral law.
     a. Reason participating in eternal law (CCC, nos. 1954-1955).
     b. Basis for human rights and duties (CCC, no. 1956).
     c. Found in all cultures, basis for moral rules and civil law (CCC, nos. 1958-1960).
B. Revelation.
  1. Teachings revealed by God under the Old Covenant.
     - Context of the Ten Commandments (CCC, nos. 2052-2074).
     - Principle of interpretation (CCC, no. 2083).
     a. Ten Commandments.
        1) First Commandment: I am the LORD, your God; you shall not have strange gods before me.
           a) Theological virtues: faith, hope, and charity (CCC, nos. 2087-2094).
           b) Sins to avoid: superstition, idolatry, divination and magic, irreligion, atheism, agnosticism (CCC, nos. 2110-2132).
        2) Second Commandment: You shall not take the name of the LORD, your God, in vain.
           a) Reverent speech about God (CCC, nos. 2142-2145).
           b) Sins to avoid: blasphemy or other abuse of God's name, perjury, misusing God's name in oaths or false oaths (CCC, nos. 2146-2155).
        3) Third Commandment: Remember to keep holy the LORD's Day.
           a) Meaning of Lord's Day (CCC, nos. 2168-2176).
           b) Serious obligation to attend Mass (CCC, nos. 2180-2185).
           c) Day of grace—rest from work (CCC, nos. 2184-2188).
           d) Sins against Third Commandment: missing Mass on Sundays and holy days (CCC, nos. 2180-2182), failing to pray (CCC, nos. 2744-2745), failing to keep holy the Lord's Day (CCC, nos. 2184-2188).
        4) Fourth Commandment: Honor your father and your mother.
           a) Obedience in the family.
              (1) Context of Christian family (CCC, nos. 2201-2206).
              (2) Duties of family members (CCC, nos. 2214-2231).

- b) Duties of civil authority and duties of citizens (CCC, nos. 2234-2243).
5) Fifth Commandment: You shall not kill.
    - a) Respect human life in all its stages and situations (CCC, nos. 2258-2262).
    - b) Legitimate self-defense and the death penalty (CCC, nos. 2263-2267).
    - c) Principles regarding health, science, bodily integrity (CCC, nos. 2292-2301).
    - d) Sins against the Fifth Commandment: murder; suicide; abortion; euthanasia; embryonic stem cell research; abuse of alcohol, drugs, food, or tobacco; abuse of the body (CCC, nos. 364, 2268-2283, 2290-2291).
6) Sixth Commandment: You shall not commit adultery.
    - a) Vocation to chastity (CCC, nos. 2337-2350).
    - b) Offenses against chastity (CCC, nos. 2351-2359).
    - c) Christian vision of marriage—theology of the body (CCC, nos. 2360-2379).
    - d) Offenses against the dignity of marriage (CCC, nos. 2380-2391).
    - e) Natural family planning.
7) Seventh Commandment: You shall not steal.
    - a) Right to private property and just treatment (CCC, nos. 2401-2407).
    - b) Sins to avoid: theft, keeping something loaned or lost, the destruction of the property of others, business fraud, paying unjust wages, breaking contracts (CCC, nos. 2408-2418).
    - c) Overview of the social doctrine of the Church (CCC, nos. 2419-2449).
    - d) Economic activity and social justice (CCC, nos. 2426-2436).
    - e) Justice and solidarity among nations (CCC, nos. 2437-2442).
8) Eighth Commandment: You shall not bear false witness against another.
    - a) Living and witnessing truth (CCC, nos. 2468-2474).
    - b) Sins to avoid: lying, perjury, rash judgment, detraction, calumny, boasting, making fun of others (CCC, nos. 2475-2487).
    - c) Keeping secrets and confidences (CCC, no. 2489).
    - d) The responsibilities of the media and art (CCC, nos. 2493-2503).
9) Ninth Commandment: You shall not covet your neighbor's wife.
    - a) Respect the sanctity of marriage vows (CCC, nos. 2364-2365).
    - b) Practice modesty and purity of heart in thought, words, actions, and appearance (CCC, nos. 2517-2527).
    - c) Sins to avoid: lust and pornography (CCC, nos. 2351, 2354).
10) Tenth Commandment: You shall not covet your neighbor's goods.
    - a) Practice simplicity of life and trust in God (CCC, nos. 2541-2548).
    - b) Sins to avoid: envy and greed (CCC, nos. 2535-2540).
2. Teaching revealed by God in the New Covenant.
    a. Two Great Commandments of Jesus (CCC, no. 2083).
        1) First Great Commandment relates to the first three Commandments of the Decalogue.
        2) Second Great Commandment relates to the rest of the Decalogue.
    b. The grace of the Holy Spirit (CCC, nos. 1966, 2003).
    c. The Sermon on the Mount (CCC, nos. 1966-1970).
        1) Beatitudes: Christ's answer to the question about happiness (CCC, nos. 1716-1723).
            a) Blessed are the poor in spirit.
            b) Blessed are they who mourn.
            c) Blessed are the meek.
            d) Blessed are the merciful.
            e) Blessed are those who hunger and thirst for righteousness.
            f) Blessed are the pure in heart.
            g) Blessed are the peacemakers (CCC, nos. 2302-2317).
            h) Blessed are those who are persecuted for righteousness' sake.
        2) Other teaching.
            a) Love your enemies (CCC, no. 2844).
            b) Absolute trust in God (CCC, nos. 2828, 2861).
            c) Non-violence (defense of innocent) (CCC, nos. 2306, 2263-2265).
            d) Charity to others in judgment and action (CCC, nos. 1823-1827, 2478).
            e) Avoidance of hypocrisy (CCC, no. 579).

- C. The Church: her teaching authority and responsibility.
  1. The Magisterium (CCC, nos. 2030-2040, 888-892).
  2. Role of the law in Christian tradition (CCC, nos. 1950-1974).
  3. The Church as teacher of moral principles (CCC, nos. 2032-2035).
  4. Church law.
     a. Canon law (CCC, nos. 736-738; see CCC, Glossary).
     b. The precepts of the Church (CCC, nos. 2042-2043).
     c. Magisterium and natural law (CCC, no. 2036).
  5. Church teaching forms one's conscience for moral decision making (CCC, nos. 1776-1782, 1795-1797).

III. Living New Life in Christ Jesus and the Gospel Message Are the Basis for Catholic Moral Teaching

- A. God's love and mercy through Jesus Christ (CCC, nos. 2011, 2196, 2448).
- B. Our vocation—a universal call to holiness as disciples of Jesus Christ.
  1. Discipleship (CCC, nos. 520-521, 901-913).
     a. "Love one another as I have loved you."
     b. Discipleship—lived witness.
        1) Daily life and work.
        2) Married and unmarried.
        3) Service to the Church (CCC, no. 898).
        4) Missionary activity (CCC, nos. 904-907, 931).
        5) Religious movements (e.g., charismatic renewal).
     c. The radical demands of the Gospel for all believers.
  2. New movements which involve the laity (e.g., Focolare; Communion and Liberation).
  3. Consecrated life and societies of apostolic life (CCC, nos. 914-933).
  4. Third orders and associates; life in the Spirit (CCC, nos. 825, 1694).
- C. Grace (CCC, nos. 1996-2005).
  1. Definition.
  2. Types of grace.
- D. Virtue (CCC, no. 1803).
  1. Definition of virtue (CCC, no. 1803).
  2. Types of virtue (CCC, nos. 1804-1832).
     a. Theological virtues (CCC, nos. 1812-1829).
     b. Cardinal virtues (CCC, nos. 1804, 1810-1811).
- E. Sustaining the moral life of the Christian.
  1. Seven gifts of the Holy Spirit (CCC, nos. 1830-1831).
  2. The twelve fruits of the Holy Spirit (CCC, no. 1832).
- F. Conscience.
  1. Definition of conscience (CCC, nos. 1777-1782).
  2. Types of conscience (CCC, nos. 1785, 1790-1794).
  3. Proper formation of conscience (CCC, nos. 1783-1785).
  4. Moral responsibility of following an informed conscience (CCC, nos. 1783-1785).
  5. Freedom of conscience (CCC, no. 1782).
- G. Sacraments and prayer offer us the grace and strength to live a moral life.
  1. Baptism and Confirmation (CCC, nos. 1262-1274).
  2. Eucharist (CCC, nos. 1391-1405).
  3. Penance (CCC, nos. 1468-1484).
  4. Sacraments of Holy Orders and Matrimony (CCC, nos. 1533-1535).
  5. Prayer (CCC, nos. 2623, 2673-2677, 2700-2719).
- H. Appropriating and living the moral teaching of Jesus Christ and his Church (CCC, no. 1694).
  1. The importance of regular participation in Mass (CCC, nos. 1742, 2011, 2014, 2016).
  2. The importance of personal prayer on Jesus Christ's teachings (CCC, nos. 2014-2016).

IV. The Reality of Sin

- A. Original innocence (CCC, nos. 369-379).
- B. Effects of Original Sin (CCC, nos. 396-406).
- C. The reality of sin (CCC, nos. 1849-1869).
  1. Definition of sins of omission and commission (CCC, no. 1853).
  2. Types of sin: mortal and venial—conditions for mortal sin (CCC, nos. 1855-1860).
  3. Sins of omission (CCC, no. 1853).
  4. Sins of commission (CCC, no. 1853).
  5. Effects of sin (CCC, nos. 1861-1864).
  6. Capital sins (CCC, no. 1866).
- D. Scriptural images of sin (CCC, nos. 1852-1853, 1867).

V. Challenges

A. If God created me free, doesn't that mean that I alone can decide what is right and wrong (CCC, nos. 1776-1794, 1954-1960)?

1. No. The freedom God gave us is the capacity to choose what is right, true, and good and to resist temptation to sin (CCC, nos. 1730-1742); education for freedom (CCC, nos. 2207, 2223, 2228, 2526). The use of freedom to do whatever we want is a misuse of that freedom and actually lessens our freedom (CCC, no. 1742).
2. Freedom is following the natural law God planted in our hearts (CCC, nos. 1954-1960).
3. In reality, sinful acts diminish freedom; moral acts increase it (CCC, no. 1733).

B. Isn't it wrong to judge other people by telling them something they are doing is wrong?

1. No. We have a responsibility to each other to encourage one another to live a life free of sin. To do that, we must remember that sin is real (CCC, nos. 1849-1869) and be willing to call what is sinful "sin."
2. You would warn friends against doing something that could harm them; sin harms them more than physical evil (CCC, no. 1787).
3. The Church reminds us that we are to love the sinner, hate the sin (Jn 8:1-11; CCC, nos. 1465, 1846).
4. The pressure in society to practice tolerance toward all, no matter what they do, is a distorted understanding of what tolerance means; moral actions must always be measured by truth (CCC, nos. 2477-2478).
5. Fraternal correction is an act of charity (CCC, nos. 1793-1794).
6. Objective moral judgment prevents chaos; moral relativism is a common problem today (CCC, nos. 2488-2492).

C. Isn't it wrong for the Church to impose her views of morality on others (CCC, nos. 1949-1960)?

1. The Church has the responsibility to teach everyone as persuasively as possible about what God has revealed about how people should live, act, and treat each other; fulfilling this responsibility is not the same as the Church's imposing her own views on others. In the development of public policy, the Church promotes the universal moral law and the common good, not her own ecclesiastical disciplines (CCC, nos. 1716-1724).
2. Human dignity and the moral code revealed by God are universal, that is, meant for every person (CCC, no. 1700).
3. All people have the ability to understand the Church's basic moral teaching because God has written the natural law on the heart of every person (CCC, nos. 1954-1960).
4. If every person were to live by a relative moral code dependent on choice, this would lead to chaos and a loss of happiness.

D. Why can't we make up our own minds and be in control over everything?

1. The Church does teach that everyone can and should make up their own minds about their actions. The key is that the decision is made on the basis of an informed or educated conscience. The Church teaches us what is right and wrong to help us form our consciences correctly.
2. It is always important to remember that we are finite human beings. This means we cannot know everything and we cannot be in control of everything.
3. We have to remember that God knows, sees, and understands more than any of us can.
4. The tragic conflicts that still exist in the world point to the imperfection of human beings (CCC, no. 2317).
5. Our sinfulness can only be overcome by Christ's salvation (CCC, nos. 619-623).

E. There's an old saying about charity beginning at home. Doesn't this mean that I don't have to worry about helping anyone else until I have enough to take care of me and my family?

1. No; concern for others is always a responsibility and characteristic of a disciple of Jesus Christ.
2. In the Parable of the Widow's Mite (Mk 12:38-44; Lk 20:45–21:4), Jesus teaches us that real charity is measured not by how much one gives but by the degree of generosity with which something is given or done for another.

Electives

Option A: Sacred Scripture

The purpose of this course is to give an overview of Sacred Scripture with an introduction to the basic principles for understanding and interpreting the Bible. Because of the extent of the scriptural material, this outline will not try to cover the vast content but rather offer comments about Scripture's purpose and religious significance. Given the limits of a semester of study, it will not be possible to introduce all the books of the Bible here. But every effort is made to project a sense of the unity of the narrative for the divine plan of salvation, the presence of God's action in this record of his Revelation, and his desire to share his merciful love with us. It is suggested that for the detailed curriculum, comments on authorship, date of composition, and formation of text of each book of the Bible be drawn from introductions in the *New American Bible* or from the *Catholic Study Bible for the New American Bible*. This outline cites catechetical references from the *Catechism of the Catholic Church* (CCC), the *Compendium of the Catechism of the Catholic Church* (Compendium), and the *United States Catholic Catechism for Adults* (USCCA) for various explanations of Scripture, with the intention of integrating catechesis and Scripture.

All scripture is inspired by God and is useful for teaching, for refutation, for correction, and for training in righteousness, so that one who belongs to God may be competent, equipped for every good work. (2 Tm 3:14-17)

I. Divine Revelation: God Speaks to Us

A. God's self-Revelation in words, deeds, covenants (CCC, nos. 50-53).
  1. Stages of Revelation (the history or divine plan of salvation) (CCC, nos. 54-55).
     a. From Adam and Eve to covenant with Noah (CCC, nos. 56-58).
     b. Succeeding covenants: Abraham, Moses, and Sinai (CCC, nos. 59-61).
     c. Definitive stage of Revelation: in Word made flesh, Jesus Christ (CCC, nos. 65-67).
B. Transmission of Divine Revelation (CCC, no. 74).
  1. Message of Christ transmitted by Apostolic Tradition (CCC, nos. 75-79).
     a. Passed on by Apostles to bishops and their successors (CCC, nos. 75-79).
     b. A living Tradition and a written one in Scripture (CCC, nos. 81-83).
     c. Scripture, Tradition, Magisterium work together (Compendium, no. 17; CCC, nos. 84-85).
C. Sacred Scripture (CCC, nos. 101-133).
  1. God is author—guarantees its truth about salvation (CCC, nos. 101-108).
  2. Word of God in words of man—literary forms—schools of biblical criticism or analysis.
  3. Principles of interpretation (CCC, nos. 112-114).
  4. Canon of Scripture—forty-six books of Old Testament, twenty-seven of New (CCC, nos. 120-130).
  5. Senses of Scripture: literal; spiritual: allegorical, moral, anagogical (CCC, nos. 115-119).
  6. Role of Scripture in the life of the Church (CCC, nos. 131-133).
  7. How to use the Bible.
D. Faith is our personal and communal response to Revelation (*Compendium*, nos. 25-32; CCC, nos. 142-143).

II. The Pentateuch or Torah—First Five Books of Scripture

A. Genesis, Exodus, Leviticus, Numbers, Deuteronomy.
  1. A major theory of the formation of these books is that they rely on several sources—primarily four: Yahwist, Elohist, Priestly, Deuteronomic (J, E, P, D).
  2. Any and all parts of Scripture must be read and interpreted in relation to the whole.
B. Book of Genesis.
  1. Primeval history: 1–11—creation, Adam and Eve, the fall, promise of redemption, and effects of sin told in figurative language (CCC, nos. 337, 362, 375; *Compendium*, nos. 51-78).
  2. Faith teachings in primeval history (NAB, Introduction).

3. Call of Abraham, our father in faith (Gn 11:27–25:18).
   4. Patriarchs Isaac, Jacob, Joseph in Egypt (Gn 27:19–50:26).
C. Book of Exodus.
   1. Prominence of the call and life of Moses.
   2. Divine liberation from slavery to freedom.
   3. Passover.
   4. Sinai Covenant.
D. Leviticus, Numbers, Deuteronomy.
   1. Expansion of Israel's history.
   2. Further development of Israel's laws.
   3. Israel's liturgical practices.

III. Joshua and the Era of the Judges

A. Book of Joshua, successor to Moses, begins conquest of Promised Land.
B. Judges—God's charismatic leaders rescue Israel from enemy.
C. Story of Ruth.

IV. Historical Books

A. 1 and 2 Samuel.
   1. Samuel anoints first King of Israel—Saul's problems.
   2. Saul and David (1 Sm 16–31)—the David stories.
   3. David as King (2 Sm 1–18)—God's covenant with House of David.
B. 1 and 2 Kings.
   1. David and Solomon ruled a united Israel and Judah.
   2. Solomon (1 Kgs 1–11)—his wisdom; builder of temple.
   3. Death of Solomon—kingdom divided by civil war.
   4. Elijah: powerful prophet opposed to idolatry.
      1) Elisha receives the mantle of prophecy from Elijah.
   5. Reforming Kings: Hezekiah and Josiah.
   6. Assyria overtakes Israel/Samaria in 722 BC (2 Kgs 17).
   7. Babylon takes people into exile in 586 BC (2 Kgs 24–25).
   8. Ezra-Nehemiah: return of exiles to Judah (539 BC).
   9. Other history books: Chronicles 1–2, Tobit, Judith, Esther, Maccabees 1–2.

V. Wisdom Books

A. Wisdom literature: a collection of practical guides to human problems and questions.
B. The book of Job—the problem of suffering and Job's response.
C. Psalms: prayer of God's People, and Church's prayer (CCC, nos. 2585-2589).
D. Proverbs, Ecclesiastes, Song of Songs, Wisdom, Sirach.

VI. The Prophets

A. The purpose of prophets.
   1. Interpreted signs of the times in light of covenant.
   2. Afflicted the comfortable and comforted the afflicted.
   3. Their prophesies were medicinal, meant to convert listeners to God.
B. Isaiah (eighth century BC).
   1. Preached the holiness of God.
   2. The qualities of the Messiah and the new Jerusalem.
   3. The saving role of suffering servant.
C. Jeremiah (640-587 BC).
   1. Born of a priestly family, chosen while in womb.
   2. Preached downfall of Israel due to infidelity.
   3. His introspective temperament made him want to escape his tough calling.
D. Ezekiel (sixth century BC).
   1. Born of priestly family, deported to Babylon in 598 BC—rest of life in exile.
   2. Served as prophet to encourage the exiles.
   3. Probably started synagogues—places for teaching and prayer.
E. Daniel.
   1. Young Jewish hero from days of Babylonian exile.
   2. Not strictly a prophet, rather part of apocalyptic strain of Bible.
   3. His apocalypses influenced the writer of book of Revelation.
F. Other prophets: Hosea, Joel, Amos, Obadiah, Jonah, Micah, Nahum, Habakkuk, Zephaniah, Haggai, Zechariah, Malachi.

VII. Overview of the New Testament

A. Gospels of Matthew, Mark, Luke, and John.
B. Acts of the Apostles.
C. Letters or epistles attributed to Paul, James, Peter, John, and Jude.
D. Revelation.
E. These twenty-seven books are authoritative for Christian life and faith.

VIII. The Gospels

A. The word "Gospel" means Good News of salvation from sin and the gift of divine life.
   1. God's promise in the Old Testament is fulfilled in the Incarnation, life, teachings, Paschal Mystery of Jesus Christ.
   2. Stages in formation of Gospels (CCC, no. 125).
   3. Matthew, Mark, Luke called "Synoptic Gospels" due to similar content.
   4. John differs in content and approach.
   5. Placing the Gospels first gives the impression they were the first New Testament (NT) books to be written; but Paul's letters were written first.
   6. Non-canonical Gospels: what they are, and why they are not part of the NT.
B. Matthew.
   1. Approximate date of composition and community/audience for which it was written.
   2. First two chapters contain infancy narrative—emphasis on Joseph, on the Magi, and on genealogy back to Abraham.
   3. Central message: Kingdom of Heaven, need for repentance to welcome the Kingdom, commission of Peter as an ecclesial emphasis.
   4. Message structured in five sections introduced by Christ's discourses (to parallel the five books of the Torah).
   5. Passion and Resurrection narratives—majestic salvation accounts.
   6. Great commission—the call to evangelization.
C. Mark.
   1. Approximate date of composition and community/audience for which it was written.
   2. Shortest Gospel.
   3. Becoming a disciple of Christ is his major theme.
   4. Passion account is prominent.
   5. Reveals Christ's divinity through reactions of people to Christ's miracles and teachings with amazement, wonder, awe, astonishment, but above all at the Cross; all titles of Christ acquire best meaning in his saving Death.
D. Luke.
   1. Approximate date of composition and community/audience for which it was written.
   2. Opens with an infancy narrative that focuses on Mary's role and the adoration of the shepherds (and genealogy back to Adam).
   3. Themes: Gospel of pardons and mercy; for the poor; of prayer and Holy Spirit; of concern for women.
   4. Passion account—God's will is accomplished. Resurrection narratives include Emmaus journey, breaking of bread.
E. John.
   1. Approximate date of composition and community/audience for which it was written.
   2. John begins with the Word of God made flesh who dwells among us.
   3. Book of seven signs and explanatory discourses (chapters 2–11).
   4. Book of glory (Jn 18–21): Jesus is "lifted up" on the Cross and "lifted up" from the tomb to everlasting glory.
   5. I AM statements: Jesus appropriates God's title at burning bush.
   6. Priestly prayer of Jesus (chapters 12–17).
   7. Caution against misusing John's texts for anti-Semitism (*Nostra Aetate*, no. 4).

IX. Acts of the Apostles

A. Revelation of Holy Spirit, who manifests, teaches, and guides Church.
   1. Catechesis on Holy Spirit (*Compendium*, nos. 136-146).
   2. Nine days of prayer for coming of Spirit—Mary in center of disciples.
B. The infant Church—*communio* (Acts 2:42-47).
C. Stories of Peter (Acts 1–12): "No other name," Stephen, Cornelius.
D. Stories of Paul (Acts 13–28): conversion; Jerusalem council; ministers of the Word; missionary journeys.

X. The Letters

A. The Letter to the Romans.
   1. Longest and most systematic example of Paul's thinking on the Gospel of God's righteousness that saves all who believe (NAB, Introduction).

2. Powerful teaching about the lordship of Christ and the need for faith in him in order to be saved.
3. Paul pleads with all Christians to hold fast to faith.
4. Justification (Rom 6–8).
5. Catechesis on justification and faith (*Compendium*, nos. 422-428).
6. Need for preaching Gospel so people hear call to faith (Rom 14:1-21).

B. The First Letter to the Corinthians.
1. Filled with information about the Church of first generation.
2. Paul addresses a number of pastoral issues.
   a. Questions of apostolic authority.
   b. Abuses at house liturgies.
   c. How to deal with gift of tongues.
   d. Eating meat sacrificed to idols.
   e. Marriage after death of spouse.
   f. Factions in the community.
3. Paul develops teachings about
   a. The Eucharist—consistent with Tradition: "I received from the Lord what I also handed on to you . . ." (1 Cor 11:23).
   b. Gifts of the Holy Spirit—the greatest being love (*agape*).
   c. The mystery of the Resurrection of Christ and of the dead.

C. Other New Testament letters: 2 Corinthians, Galatians, Ephesians, Philippians, Colossians, 1–2 Thessalonians, 1–2 Timothy, Titus, Philemon, Hebrews, 1–2 Peter, 1–3 John, Jude.

XI. Book of Revelation

A. This book is fundamentally about Christ's in-breaking into history and the world's fight against him and his followers.

B. Written to encourage the faith of seven churches (chapters 2–3), which were subject to harassment and persecution from Jewish and Roman authorities. These churches also suffered from internal disorder, false teaching, and apathy.

C. Use of apocalyptic language—borrowed from Ezekiel and Daniel.
1. In 404 verses there are 278 allusions to Old Testament—no direct quotes.
2. This book is not intended to be an exact prediction of future historical events.
3. Apocalyptic language was part of the literary genre of this time and culture.

D. John on Patmos receives call from vision of Christ to help churches.

E. John uses crisis imagery to prophesy final mysterious transformation of world at end of history, "a new heaven and a new earth" (Rev 21:1-4).

XII. Challenges

A. Why do Catholics believe in things that are not found in the Bible?
1. The Church and her members understand that God's Revelation has come down to us in ways that are not limited to the Bible. Besides the Bible, matters of faith revealed to us by God have also been passed down through Tradition. Oral tradition preceded and accompanied the writing of the New Testament.
2. For example, many of our beliefs about Mary are not explicitly taught in the Bible but are implicitly present; they have been passed down beginning at the time of the Apostles and have been consistently reflected in the prayer and belief of the Church.

B. Why isn't Scripture enough for Catholics?
1. The Catholic Church and her members know that Scripture is important, but it is not the only way God's Revelation has been passed down to us. The Church existed more than a generation before the New Testament writings began to appear.
2. The doctrine of "*sola scriptura*" or "Scripture alone," which is espoused by a number of Protestant churches, is not found in Scripture or the teaching of the Lord Jesus.
3. St. John (Jn 21:25) writes that Scripture does not contain everything about Christ. The First Letter to Timothy (1 Tm 3:15) says that the Church is the pillar and foundation of truth.

C. Why does the Catholic Bible have more books?
1. The Septuagint, a Greek translation of the Old Testament, was in use among Christians before the rabbinical council at Jamnia opted to use the Hebrew translation only (AD 96).
2. The Septuagint contains seven additional books and additional passages in the book of Daniel and the book of Esther not in the Hebrew translation.
3. The early Christians did not change the version they used because they no longer accepted the authority of the Jewish rabbis.

Option B: History of the Catholic Church

Course Four presented a catechesis of the Church and the Body of Christ in history: its nature and meaning, images, marks, life and ministry, guide to moral life, and the role of prayer. This elective can supplement that catechesis on the Church. The purpose of this course is to supply the students with a general knowledge of the Church's history from apostolic times to the present. They will be introduced to the fact that the Church was founded by Christ through the Apostles and is sustained by him throughout history through the Holy Spirit. The students will come to know that the Church is the living Body of Christ today and, as such, has both divine and human elements. In this course, students will learn about the Church's 2,000 years of history and about how the Church is led and governed by the successors of the Apostles.

I. Christ Established His Church to Continue His Saving Presence and Work

A. The origin, foundation, and manifestation of the Church.
   1. Church planned by the Father (LG, no. 2; CCC, no. 759).
   2. Church instituted by Christ who (CCC, nos. 748, 763-766)
      a. Inaugurated the Church by preaching Good News.
      b. Endowed his community with a structure.
      c. Gave the Church totally of himself for our salvation.
   3. Church is revealed by Holy Spirit: fifty-day preparation for Pentecost (CCC, nos. 767-768).
      a. The events of the first Pentecost.
      b. The Holy Spirit's charisms in Church's life (1 Cor 12–14).
B. Holy Spirit inspires the Apostles' mission—great commission (Mt 28:16-20; CCC, nos. 857-860).
   1. The missionary journeys of St. Paul.
   2. The role of Peter and the Apostles in the early Church.
   3. Apostolic Succession preserves the mission, office, and teaching of the Apostles as entrusted to them by Christ (CCC, nos. 857-862).

II. History of Church in Post-Apostolic Times

1. An Age of Growth amid Persecution

A. Unique phenomenon in Roman Empire.
   1. Empire was tolerant in principle but changed regarding Christians who denied Roman gods and refused to worship them.
   2. "Blood of martyrs is the seed of the Church" (Tertullian [catacombs]).
   3. Teachings of St. Ignatius of Antioch, St. Justin Martyr, and St. Irenaeus sustained the faith of the persecuted Church.
B. House liturgies—Eucharist is heart of early Christian worship.
   1. Transition from Last Supper to Breaking of Bread.
   2. Development of Liturgy of the Word and of Eucharistic Prayer.
   3. Descriptions in the *Didache*; St. Justin Martyr (*Liturgy of the Hours*, Vol. II, p. 694).

2. The Age of the Fathers of the Church

A. Constantine and Edict of Milan.
   1. Freedom of worship.
   2. From house liturgies to worship in public.
      a. Building of churches for Mass and celebrations of sacraments.
      b. Sense of transcendence of God in stately settings.
B. Fathers inculturated Scripture for Greek and Roman peoples (CCC, nos. 76, 688).
   1. Influenced by Plato's philosophy through Plotinus.
   2. With sermons and commentaries on Scripture and sacraments.
      a. Preaching was a powerful means for catechesis and evangelization.
      b. Fathers and doctors of Church include St. Basil, St. Gregory Nazienzen, St. John Chrysostom, St. Athanasius, St. Ephrem, St. Ambrose, St. Jerome, St. Augustine, St. Leo the Great, St. Gregory the Great. *(N.B. Lives of saints should be mentioned throughout this course both to show the restoration of faith and hope in times of crisis as well as to illustrate ways of encountering Christ through all periods of Church history.)*
C. The development of the Eastern Patriarchates.
   1. These were located in Jerusalem, Antioch, Constantinople, and Alexandria.
   2. The See of Peter in Rome in relation to the Patriarchates.

D. Church councils and doctrinal development (CCC, nos. 9, 192, 250, 884, 887, 891).
   1. Church response to heresies (Arianism and Nestorianism): Nicea, AD 325; First Constantinople, 381; Ephesus, 431; Chalcedon, 451; and three later councils.
      a. Creeds and catechesis for Christian instruction.
   2. Dealt with doctrines of Incarnation and the Trinity.
   3. Some Eastern Churches began separating over doctrinal disputes; the first separation occurred in 431, the second in 451, and the third in 1054.

3. **The Roman Church of the West**
A. Collapse of Roman Empire of the West around 476.
   1. Barbarian invasions; weakened government.
   2. Political influence of popes and bishops increased.
      a. Church was the remaining trusted authority.
      b. Helped maintain law and order amid the encroaching invaders.
      c. Assisted with protection of civilians and feeding the poor.
B. The monks as evangelizers.
   1. St. Benedict and the Benedictines.
   2. St. Columban and the Celtic monks.
      a. Brought Christ and Church to northern Europe.
      b. Developed agriculture, wool production, vineyards.
      c. Stabilized the nomadic tribes and gave birth to towns.
      d. Monastic schools promoted education, culture, and classics.

4. **The Church of the Middle Ages**
A. Politics and religion.
   1. Charlemagne's Frankish Empire.
   2. Clashes between Church and monarchies on selection of bishops.
   3. Gregory VII—Hildebrand and Gregorian reform.
B. New religious orders, new universities.
   1. Bernard and the Cistercians.
   2. Rise of the mendicant orders.
   3. Universities: Oxford, Cambridge, Paris, Padua, Krakow, etc.
   4. *Summa* of St. Thomas Aquinas.
   5. *The Imitation of Christ*, by Thomas à Kempis.
   6. Gothic cathedrals.
   7. Heresy about Eucharist—response at Council of Lateran IV.
   8. Rise of Eucharistic adoration and Feast of Corpus Christi.
   9. Saints: Clare, Francis, Gertrude, Margaret of Scotland, Dominic, Catherine of Siena, Albert the Great, Joan of Arc.
   10. Black Death cast somber pall over Christian piety.
   11. Great Schism and the Avignon Papacy.

5. **The Crusades**
A. Situating the Crusades.
   1. Islam's birth and its first encounters with Christianity.
   2. Shrines in the Holy Land fall under Islam's control.
   3. Christian military response.
   4. Success and failure of Crusades (attacks on Jews).
B. Some results of the Crusades.
   1. Cultural and economic resurgence of Europe.
   2. Tensions between East and West.

6. **The Renaissance: Return to Sources**
A. Scholars.
   1. Erasmus and Thomas More.
   2. Revival of study of classical culture and languages.
   3. Christian humanism—new translation of Bible.
B. Art and architecture and music.
   1. Florence and the Medicis, patrons of arts and schools.
   2. Fra Angelico, Giotto, Raphael, Michelangelo, Bramante, Bernini.
   3. The new St. Peter's Basilica, Sistine Chapel, *Duomo* in Florence.
   4. St. Philip Neri, Apostle of Rome, promoted the music of Palestrina and historical scholarship of Baronius.

7. **The Call for Reform**
A. Luther's complaints and proposals; innovations.
   1. Sale of indulgences, clerical corruption, ignorance of the faith.
   2. *Sola Fides, Sola Gratia, Sola Scriptura*.
   3. Use of printing press, catechism, vernacular Bible and liturgy, married clergy, Eucharist under two species, lay priesthood.
B. The break from Rome: Protestantism.
   1. Martin Luther (Germany).
   2. John Calvin, Huldrych Zwingli (Switzerland).
   3. Henry VIII (England).
   4. John Knox (Scotland).

C. Nationalism.
   1. Thirty Years' War between Catholics and Protestants.
   2. *Cuius Regio–Eius Religio*—rise of state churches.
D. Church responds at the Council of Trent.
   1. Renewal of bishops, priests, religious.
   2. Doctrinal and pastoral issues.
      a. Role of grace and good works.
      b. Sacrificial character of the Mass (CCC, nos. 1362-1372).
      c. Real Presence of Christ in Eucharist—Transubstantiation (CCC, no. 1376).
      d. Seminaries and proper formation of priests.
      e. A universal catechism.
E. Counter-reform.
   1. Mass of St. Pius V, Roman catechism, Jesuit education.
   2. Baroque architecture and concert-style Masses—symbolized the newfound confidence of the Church.
   3. Saints: Ignatius, Robert Bellarmine, Peter Canisius, Teresa of Avila, John of the Cross, Charles Borromeo, Francis de Sales, Jane de Chantal, Vincent de Paul, Louise de Marillac.

8. **The Age of Exploration: Church's Missionaries Confront New Cultures**
A. The Americas.
   1. St. Peter Claver's ministry to African slaves.
   2. Conversion of Mexico: Our Lady of Guadalupe—St. Juan Diego.
   3. St. Rose of Lima and St. Martin de Porres.
   4. North American martyrs—Church in American colonies.
B. Missionaries (Jesuits, Franciscans, Dominicans).
C. Japan, India—St. Francis Xavier.
D. Matteo Ricci, SJ (attempted inculturation in China).

9. **The Age of Enlightenment**
A. Rationalism, scientific model, Deism—Descartes, Voltaire, Rousseau.
B. The French Revolution and its impact on the Church.
C. Post-revolutionary France saw religious revival in nineteenth century.
   1. New religious congregations founded for teaching.
   2. St. Bernadette's vision of Mary at Lourdes—pilgrimage site.
   3. Saints: Therese of Lisieux, Margaret Mary Alacoque, John Vianney, Catherine Laboure.

10. **Vatican I**
A. Pope Pius IX reigned thirty-two years, 1846-1878.
   1. Strengthened spiritual authority of Pope after loss of Papal States.
   2. Man of deep faith and virtues, beatified in 2000.
   3. His *Syllabus of Errors*.
   4. Immaculate Conception dogma, 1854 (CCC, nos. 490-493).
B. The First Vatican Council.
   1. Opened December 8, 1869—306 years after Council of Trent.
   2. First discussion: Dogmatic Constitution on Faith.
      a. Council fathers approved document *Dei Filius*.
      b. Reason can know God—but Revelation is necessary.
   3. July 1870: infallibility of Pope defined (CCC, nos. 889-891, 2035, 2051).
   4. August 1870: Papal States occupied; pope suspended Council.

11. **Industrial Revolution—Need for Social Justice for Workers (1878-1903)**
A. Industrial Revolution.
B. Social injustices.
   1. No living wage, no pensions or sick leave; child labor, sweat shops.
   2. Denial of right to form labor unions or mount strikes.
   3. Management's ignoring human dignity of workers, etc.
C. Pope Leo XIII (1878-1903)—*Rerum Novarum*.
   1. Universal destination of goods of earth for all people.
   2. Subsidiarity, justice for workers, reform of capitalism (CCC, nos. 1883, 1885, 1894, 2209).
   3. Common good, private property, living wage, unions (CCC, nos. 1807, 2401, 2403, 2246, 2435).

12. **The Church and Social Justice Teaching**
A. Pope Leo XIII, *Rerum Novarum*.
B. Pope Pius XI, *Quadragesimus Anno*.
C. Pope John XXIII, *Mater et Magistra, Pacem in Terris*.
D. Second Vatican Council, *Gaudium et Spes*.
E. Pope Paul VI, *Populorum Progressio, Octogesima Adveniens*.
F. Pope John Paul II, *Laborem Exercens, Sollicitudo Rei Socialis, Centesimus Annus*.
G. United States Conference of Catholic Bishops, *The Challenge of Peace, Economic Justice for All*.

13. **Pope St. Pius X (1903-1914)**
   A. Motto "To Restore All Things in Christ."
      1. Lowered age of First Communion to age of reason.
      2. Popularized Gregorian chant—helped liturgical movement.
   B. Opposed "modernism."

14. **The Church and the World Wars**
   A. Pope Benedict XV and World War I—seven-point peace plan.
   B. Pope Pius XI.
      1. Signed Lateran Treaty with Mussolini; broke with Mussolini in 1931.
      2. His break with Hitler—encyclical *Mit Brennender Sorge*.
   C. Pope Pius XII.
      1. Opposed Nazis; Christmas messages for peace.
      2. Pius and the Jews—his efforts to protect them.
      3. Spiritual signs of light in darkness of war and its aftermath—1954 proclaimed dogma of the Assumption—encyclicals.

15. **Vatican Council II: A Pastoral Approach to the World**
   A. Pope John XXIII—his pastoral vision for the Council (see his opening speech at Council: *Gaudet Mater Ecclesia* [*Rejoice, O Mother Church*], October 11, 1962).
   B. The Council documents—pastoral tone and language.
   C. Pope Paul VI (1963).
      1. Guided remaining sessions of Council.
      2. Implemented Council teachings.
      3. Controversy over *Humanae Vitae*.
      4. Met with Athenagoras in Istanbul.
      5. Visits to New York, Bombay, Manila, etc.
      6. Promoted synods of bishops.
      7. Succeeded by Pope John Paul I, who reigned thirty-three days.
   D. Some developments after the Council.
      1. Changes in liturgy, growth of Scripture study, new look in church architecture, growth of lay involvement—parish councils, etc.
      2. Liturgical movement, work by Catholic Action, and work by Scripture scholars preceded Council and enabled its implementation.
      3. Developments in catechesis; understanding the need for both content and formation.
      4. Call to evangelization—*Evangelii Nuntiandi*.
      5. Renewal of the Eastern Churches.

16. **Pope John Paul II: The Church Looks to the Twenty-First Century**
   A. First non-Italian pope in centuries—vigorous, dramatic, faced down Communism.
   B. Evangelizer to the world: 104 papal trips overseas, his *Dialogue of Salvation*.
   C. Teacher: numerous encyclicals, post-synodal documents, writings.
      1. *Fides et Ratio*, *Evangelium Vitae*, *Veritatis Splendor*.
      2. Wednesday talks on Genesis—theology of the body.
   D. Pastor: Holy Thursday letters to priests—his World Youth Days.
   E. Themes: be not afraid; Mary, *Totus Tuus*; human dignity, new evangelization.
   F. Assassination attempt: example of courage, faith, and forgiveness.
   G. The *Catechism of the Catholic Church*.

17. **Pope Benedict XVI**
   A. First encyclical *Deus Caritas Est* followed by apostolic exhortation *Sacramentum Caritatis*.
   B. Addresses clash of culture and civilization with faith.
   C. Ecumenism today: Church of the East, Oriental Orthodox, Eastern Orthodox, Protestant.

18. **The Church in the United States**
   A. Colonial America.
      1. French-speaking Catholics—Jesuit explorers, missions, martyrs.
      2. Spanish-speaking Catholics—Junipero Serra, etc.
      3. English colonial Catholics—Archbishop John Carroll.
   B. Immigrations—ethnic Catholics.
      1. Second-class citizens; Church supports working class.
      2. Catholic school and hospital systems—religious orders.
      3. Parish as center of social life; patriotism gains acceptance.
   C. Church's role in development of social justice in the United States.
      1. Cardinal Gibbons and implementation of the Church teaching on workers in the late nineteenth and early twentieth century.
      2. Church support of labor unions' fight for rights of workers.
      3. The Depression and its effects.

D. Eastern Catholics.
   1. Establishment of hierarchies.
   2. Presence today.
E. Catholic education.
   1. Rise of parochial schools and education of children and youth.
   2. Efforts in higher education; significant percentage of the world's Catholic colleges and universities are found in the United States.
   3. High percentage of university-educated followers helped Catholics become members of middle and upper-middle class.
   4. Contribution of Catholic schools in modern urban settings.
F. Late twentieth to start of twenty-first century.
   1. Areas for concern.
      a. Birth control, legalization of abortion.
      b. Priest sex abuse crisis; confidence in Church blurred.
      c. Church attendance and vocations to priesthood and religious life decline.
      d. Rapid secularization of society and breakdown of the family.
      e. Religious illiteracy.
   2. Reasons for hope.
      a. Impact of the papacy of Pope John Paul II—leadership, evangelization.
      b. Pro-life movement—adult stem cell research and benefits.
      c. Regrowth of seminaries and new religious communities.
      d. Influence of the *Catechism of the Catholic Church*.
      e. Multiple forms of lay leadership—less polarization.
      f. Rise of youth and young adult activities in the Church: World Youth Days.
      g. American saints: Elizabeth Seton, Frances Cabrini, John Neumann, Katharine Drexel, Rose Philippine Duchesne, Theodora Guerin; Blessed Junipero Serra, Blessed Kateri Tekakwitha.

III. Challenges

A. How can the Church claim to be holy and a protector of truth when there are things in her history like the Crusades, the Inquisition, the persecution of Jews, and the Galileo case?
   1. The Church is a source and means of holiness for people because God has made it so. The failures of the Church's members during her history are lamentable. The virtuous lives of the saints validate the truth and power of the Church's sacraments and teaching.
   2. Though the members of the Church are prone to sin, the Church herself is sinless and holy.
   3. Despite the sins of her members, including the ordained, the Church is entrusted by God with the truth of the Gospel and the graced means of salvation.
   4. Many members of the Church are also holy and possess a heroic sanctity witnessed to by the countless sacrifices many have made, often to the point of martyrdom.
   5. Pope John Paul II, on various occasions, apologized for the sins of the members of the Church in her history, including for harm caused by the excesses of the Inquisition and atrocities committed during the Crusades.
   6. The historical context in which these events happened: the people of those days dealt differently with threats and problems than we might do so now. They used means that were commonly used in their society then. We cannot judge them as harshly as some people judge them today.
B. If the Catholic Church truly has the fullness of truth, why have other churches broken away from her?
   1. Generally, other churches broke away from the Catholic Church because of some human element such as a disagreement with how beliefs are expressed or explained, or a desire to change forms of worship, or political or personal reasons. While the Church has the fullness of truth, not all her members appropriate and live that fullness of truth.
   2. Other breaks from the Catholic Church were the result of impatience on the part of those who saw a need for reform or a problem they wished to address.
   3. The Catholic Church is committed to seek unity in faith, and she works toward that, but such work for unity cannot compromise the truth of the faith.

Option C: Living as a Disciple of Jesus Christ in Society

The purpose of this course is to introduce students to the Church's social teaching. In this course, students are to learn how Christ's concern for others, especially the poor and needy, is present today in the Church's social teaching and mission.

I. God's Plan for His People

Vatican II: The Church is a sign and instrument of communion with God and the unity of the whole human race (LG, no. 1).

A. Salvation and truth (CCC, no. 851).
   1. Redemption through the Paschal Mystery.
   2. Eternal life with the Triune God in heaven.
B. Happiness in this life (CCC, no. 1718).
   1. Happiness is a shared communion with God.
      a. Trinitarian *communio* is the pattern for social life (CCC, nos. 267, 738, 1693).
      b. Witness Christ in words and actions.
   2. The unity of the whole human race (CCC, nos. 842, 1877).
      a. The social nature of the human person (CCC, nos. 1878-1889, 1929).
      b. The need for others.
   3. The household of faith—Church as the following:
      a. Mystical Body of Christ (CCC, nos. 774-779, 787-796, 805-807, 872, 1123, 1396, 1548, 2003).
      b. Family of God (CCC, no. 2790).
      c. Community of sanctified believers (CCC, no. 824).
      d. Teacher: forms the social conscience of society.
      e. Listener: ecumenism.

II. Social Teaching of the Church

A. Church always has stood for charity and justice (CCC, no. 953).
   1. Social teachings in Scripture.
      a. Amos and Isaiah.
      b. The Sermon on the Mount; Last Judgment (CCC, nos. 2153, 2262, 2336, 2605, 2830).
      c. Communal sharing, deacons, collections for churches.
   2. Church's history of social concern.
   3. Corporal and spiritual works of mercy (CCC, no. 2447).
B. Different types of justice (CCC, nos. 2411-2412, 1807).
   1. Distributive justice (CCC, nos. 2236-2411).
   2. Legal justice.
   3. Commutative justice.
   4. Social justice (CCC, nos. 1928-1942).
C. Social teaching in the modern era.
   1. Pope Leo XIII: encyclical *Rerum Novarum* in 1891.
   2. Social doctrine encyclicals of Popes Pius XI, John XXIII, Paul VI, and John Paul II.
   3. Vatican II: *Gaudium et Spes*.
   4. *Catechism of the Catholic Church*.
   5. *Compendium of the Social Doctrine of the Church*, Vatican, 2004.
D. Principles of Catholic social teaching from the Universal Magisterium.
   1. The necessity of the moral law: the moral law provides the foundation for all social teaching by accounting for man's duties and consequent rights (CCC, nos. 1959, 2070, 2242).
   2. God is the source of all civil authority: man does not confer authority upon himself, but authority flows from God to all just governments and laws (CCC, no. 1899).
   3. The perfection of the person by the common good: man is perfected not only by private goods such as food and shelter but by "common goods" such as peace and truth that come about through his life with others in community (CCC, nos. 1905-1912, 1925-1927).
      a. Respect for and promotion of the fundamental rights of the person.
      b. Prosperity, or the development of the spiritual and temporal goods of society.
      c. The peace and security of the group and its members.
E. United States Conference of Catholic Bishops (USCCB).
   1. After World War I, the bishops of the United States began a program of social reconstruction which included teachings on minimum wage, social security, and worker participation in management.
   2. Sampling of more recent pastoral letters.
      a. *Brothers and Sisters to Us* (1979).
      b. *The Challenge of Peace: God's Promise and Our Response* (1983); *Sowing Weapons of War* (1995).

    c. *Economic Justice for All: A Pastoral Letter on Catholic Social Teaching and the U.S. Economy* (1986).
    d. Statements on capital punishment: *A Good Friday Appeal to End the Death Penalty* (1999); *A Culture of Life and the Penalty of Death* (2005).

III. Major Themes of Catholic Social Teaching (CCC, nos. 1877-1948, 2196-2257)

A. The dignity of human life.
 1. All human life created and redeemed by God is sacred.
 2. Dignity due to being an image and likeness of God.
 3. The Incarnation: Jesus' identification with each of us (e.g., Mt 25:45, Acts 9:4).
B. Call to family, community, and participation.
 1. What is a family (CCC, nos. 2202-2203)?
 2. The family: foundation of society; needs support.
 3. Society should protect dignity and growth of family.
 4. All people should participate in society—work for common good.
C. Responsibilities and rights.
 1. All have right to life and to what sustains it.
 2. Society should foster and protect these rights.
 3. Responsibilities undergird human rights.
D. Preferential option for the poor.
 1. Moral principle: universal destination of the goods of the earth (CCC, nos. 2402-2406).
 2. Goods of the earth for every human being.
 3. Why all need these goods (CCC, no. 2402).
 4. See Christ in homeless, outcast, unpopular.
 5. Appropriate use of wealth and other resources.
    a. Be a voice for the voiceless.
    b. Assess social acts and their impacts on poor.
 6. Concern for the spiritually poor.
E. Dignity of work and the rights of workers.
 1. God's creation plan includes work.
 2. Right to work in just conditions.
F. Solidarity: individuals should work for the common good (CCC, nos. 2437-2442).
G. Stewardship of God's creation (CCC, nos. 2415-2418).

IV. Sin and Its Social Dimensions

A. Concept of social sin.
 1. Difference between "social sin" and personal sin (CCC, nos. 1868-1869).
    a. Personal sin at the root of social sin.
    b. Social sin stems from collective personal sins.
       1) Personal sin that contributes to social injustice.
       2) Personal choices in response to social injustice.
 2. Foundations for social sin.
    a. Attitudes that foster unjust treatment.
    b. Social structures which foster unjust treatment of others.
    c. Social sin can be passed on to future generations.
B. The social dimension of the Commandments.
 1. First three Commandments—relationship with God (CCC, nos. 2084-2195).
    a. Duty and the right to freely worship God.
    b. Societal authorities should ensure freedom of worship.
 2. The last seven Commandments focus on our relationship with others: the moral teaching of our faith must be brought into people's interaction with each other (N.B. [1] positive aspects of commandment, [2] failures to live it).
    a. Fourth Commandment (CCC, nos. 2197-2257).
       1) Respect legitimate civil authority, government care for citizens' rights, citizens' participation in public life, conscientious objection to unjust laws.
       2) Anarchy, civil unrest, corrupt government, ignoring of common good, non-participation in democratic society.
    b. Fifth Commandment (CCC, nos. 2258-2330).
       1) Fosters a civilization of life and love.
       2) Dishonor human life—culture of death.
          a) Abortion, euthanasia, physician-assisted suicide, cloning, genetic manipulation.
          b) Teaching on capital punishment.
          c) War (conditions for just war), conscientious objection.
          d) Scandal.

c. Sixth Commandment (CCC, nos. 2331-2400).
      1) Promote chaste life and love in society, marriage, family.
      2) Adultery, fornication, masturbation, homosexual acts, rape, prostitution, pornography (CCC, nos. 2351-2356).
   d. Seventh Commandment (CCC, nos. 2401-2463).
      1) Just sharing of goods, qualified right to private property, just treatment of workers, stewardship for environment, just economic policies.
      2) Stealing, unjust damage to others' property, destruction of environment, enslavement of women and children, white-collar crime, violation of public trust, perpetuation of third-world poverty.
   e. Eighth Commandment (CCC, nos. 2464-2513).
      1) Promote truth in society and media.
      2) Lies, detraction, perjury, rash judgment, violation of professional secrets.
      3) Seal of confession.
   f. Ninth Commandment (CCC, nos. 2514-2533).
      1) Create conditions for chaste life and love.
      2) Media, advertising, and exploitation of lust; "adult" bookstores, Internet pornography.
   g. Tenth Commandment (CCC, nos. 2534-2557).
      1) Make simplicity of life desirable.
      2) Cultural attitudes that idealize wealth, materialism.
C. Social dimensions of the Beatitudes (CCC, nos. 1720-1729).
   1. Blessed are the poor in spirit.
      a. Choose a lifestyle that benefits those most in need.
      b. Otherwise we will tend to materialism, selfishness, exploitation of others.
   2. Blessed are they who mourn.
      a. Be compassionate to those in pain.
      b. Loss of care for the living and defenseless.
   3. Blessed are the meek.
      a. Self-discipline in the face of evil; gentleness, unselfishness.
      b. Prone to arrogance and disrespect for others, violence.
   4. Blessed are the merciful.
      a. Forgive one another. Be quick to ask forgiveness.
      b. Holding grudges; growth in bitterness.
   5. Blessed are those who hunger and thirst for righteousness.
      a. Develop a social conscience.
      b. Indifference to mistreatment of others.
   6. Blessed are the pure in heart.
      a. Work on virtues of modesty and chastity.
      b. Lust expressed in many ways.
   7. Blessed are the peacemakers.
      a. In God's will is our peace. Perform works of peace.
      b. A divider, troublemaker, warmonger.
   8. Blessed are those who are persecuted for righteousness' sake.
      a. Witness to Jesus and the Church always; defend the innocent, even die for your faith.
      b. Cowardice, betrayal, moral compromise.
D. The two Great Commandments: love God with all of your heart, soul, and mind, and love your neighbor as yourself (Mt 22:36-40).

V. Challenges

A. Why shouldn't we look out for ourselves first? No one else will look out for me.
   1. God looks out for every human being. He brings us into being, watches over us in life, and draws us to want to live with him forever. Evidence of his concern can be found in the care for one's well-being often seen in the action of the Church as well as coming from family, friends, and members of communities to which we belong.
   2. Living in a self-centered way is one of the effects of Original Sin. God created us to live and act in a way that is centered on him and on others, not ourselves.
   3. Selflessness, rather than selfishness, is the characteristic of a disciple of Jesus Christ, who is the living embodiment of what it means to live in a selfless way.
B. Isn't the degree of a person's success and achievement really measured in terms of financial security and wealth?
   1. While there are many people who build their lives on such an approach, Jesus Christ, in his life and his teaching, teaches us that the greatest achievement is growth in holiness and virtue and becoming more like him.
   2. Real happiness is found in fulfilling God's plan for us.
   3. True and lasting fulfillment is never found in money or material possessions.

4. People who find the fulfillment in life which leads to inner peace and joy are those mature enough to understand that what really matters is God's infinite love for us and what he has taught us about himself and the meaning of life.

C. Isn't not fighting back or getting even with someone who hurts or offends you a sign of weakness?
1. No. It takes a lot more courage and strength to forgive and not seek vengeance than to fight back or try to get even.
2. Jesus Christ, in his life and his teaching, challenges us to see the truth that power and strength are to be measured in terms of virtue and inner strength.
3. We have the example of Jesus Christ, who in not fighting back and in forgiving his executioners showed true strength.
4. We have the example of the martyrs, which shows the strength and power that faith and God's grace give.

D. Isn't it more important to work for justice than to engage in charity?
1. The works of justice do not exclude the works of charity or vice versa.
2. Charity should shape justice to make it Christian; charity is not extra or optional.
3. A perfect world cannot be built by human effort for justice.
4. Perfect justice will be realized only in eternal life.

Option D: Responding to the Call of Jesus Christ

The purpose of this course is to help students to understand the vocations of life: how Christ calls us to live. In this course, students should learn how all vocations are similar and how they differ. The course should be structured around married life, single life, priestly life, and consecrated life. Students should learn what it means to live life for the benefit of others and the value in considering a vocation in service to the Christian community.

I. God's Call to Each of Us

A. Universal call to holiness (CCC, nos. 2013-2014, 2028, 2813).
  1. A longing for God is inherent to the human person.
  2. God wants every person to know him, to love him, and to serve him.
  3. How we reflect Trinitarian life.
  4. How Christ shows us the way to discipleship.
  5. The ways in which God sanctifies us.
  6. Learning how to make a gift of oneself.
B. The personal call.
  1. Our vocation from God (CCC, Glossary).
  2. A vocation is not the same as a job or career.
     a. The relationship between one's work and vocation.
  3. Definition/description of discernment—role of Church and individual.
     a. Divine Providence in the events of one's life.
     b. Prayerful reflection and discernment.
  4. Traditionally recognized states of life (CCC, nos. 2004, 2230).
     a. Married (CCC, no. 1535).
     b. Committed single life (CCC, nos. 898-900, 2442).
     c. Ordained bishop, priest, or deacon (CCC, nos. 1578, 1593).
     d. Consecrated life (CCC, nos. 916, 933).
  5. Lay ecclesial movements and ministries (CCC, nos. 901-913).
  6. No vocation is lived in isolation (CCC, nos. 543, 804, 831, 1886, 1878-1885).
     a. Human beings exist in relationship with others; give of oneself in order to find oneself.
     b. There are many levels and types of relationship.

II. "Serve One Another"

A. Teaching and example of Jesus—his commandment of love (CCC, no. 1823).
  1. An unselfish gift of self to God and others.
  2. Service to our brothers and sisters in the Church and world.
B. Sacraments at the service of Communion (CCC, nos. 1533-1535).
  1. Marriage as a sacrament given to foster the good of the human family, society, and the Church (CCC, nos. 1601-1666).
  2. Holy Orders as a sacrament given to foster the good of the spiritual family, the Church (CCC, nos. 1536-1600).

III. Sacrament of Marriage

A. God is author of marriage, which Jesus raised to a sacrament; it is not a purely human institution (CCC, nos. 1603, 1601).
  1. Book of Genesis account.
  2. Teaching on marriage in the New Testament (CCC, no. 1615).
     a. Jesus' first public sign or miracle took place at a marriage (Jn 2:1-11; CCC, no. 1613).
     b. Two shall become as one flesh; and the question on divorce (Mt 19; CCC, no. 1614).
     c. The love of husbands and wives reflecting the love of Christ for the Church (Eph 5; CCC, no. 1616).
  3. Theology of the body.
B. Christian marriage is a lifelong commitment between a baptized man and a baptized woman as husband and wife, designed to reflect the unending love that God has for his people, individually and collectively; a covenant of love (CCC, no. 1625).
  1. Encouraging signs of Christ's saving work in marriage and the family.
     a. Greater awareness of personal freedom and interpersonal relationships.
     b. Promotes the dignity of both men and women (CCC, nos. 1646-1651).
     c. Increased concern for responsible procreation; natural family planning (CCC, nos. 1652-1654).
     d. Education of children and extended family support (CCC, nos. 1603-1605).

- e. Mutual self-giving within marriage and family serves as basis for responsible activity in society and in the Church.
2. Problems encountered in marriage and family life (CCC, nos. 2331-2359).
    a. Exaggeration of the independence of the spouses to the loss of mutual dependence and becoming two in one flesh (FC, no. 6; CCC, nos. 1606-1608).
    b. Scourge of abortion, recourse to sterilization, contraceptive mentality (CCC, nos. 2270-2274, 2370, 2399).
    c. Cohabitation and homosexual union as a devaluation of the true meaning of marriage (CCC, nos. 2353-2359).
    d. Growing number of divorces (CCC, nos. 1644-1645, 1649-1650).
C. Celebration of the sacrament.
    1. Marriage: a public act that requires a liturgical celebration (CCC, nos. 1621-1623).
    2. For Roman Catholics—setting for a valid marriage.
        a. In the Latin Church the spouses are ministers of the sacrament.
        b. Role of free consent, and witness of bishop, priest, deacon.
        c. The essential three promises of the spouses.
        d. In the Eastern Churches, the bishop or priest confers the Sacrament of Matrimony.
    3. In Latin Church, the Nuptial Mass—or just the Liturgy of the Word (see *Directory for the Application of Principles and Norms on Ecumenism*, no. 159).
    4. A Catholic is encouraged to marry another Catholic (CCC, nos. 1633-1637).
        a. Permission can be given to marry those who are not Catholic.
        b. Conditions for this permission to marry non-Catholic: Catholic party promises to maintain the practice of his or her faith and to raise any children they have in the Catholic faith.
D. Preparation for receiving the sacrament (CCC, no. 1622; FC, no. 66).
    1. Remote preparation begins as children, through example of parents, relatives, and other members of the community.
    2. Proximate preparation comes through education.
        a. Need for healthy self-understanding including sexuality.
        b. Sexuality part of our being; we relate through personhood that includes sexuality.
        c. God made man and woman with a natural complementarity (see Genesis: both creation accounts).
        d. God decreed that sexual intimacy be reserved for marriage.
        e. Marriage involves a total self-giving of the spouses; requires a sense of discipline, generosity, and an understanding of true love.
        f. Expressions of healthy sexual relations in marriage.
            1) Natural family planning.
            2) Arguments against contraception.
        g. Healthy personal and dating habits as a high-school-aged person.
        h. Marriage reflects Christ's relationship to the Church (Eph 5:21-33; CCC, no. 1642).
        i. Develop skills for living a lifelong commitment.
    3. Immediate preparation.
        a. Church's responsibility to prepare couples for marriage.
        b. Dioceses require period of preparation that varies by diocese.
        c. Focus on the couples' promises.
            1) Lifelong union.
            2) Exclusive and faithful union.
            3) Openness to children.
        d. Help engaged persons grow in knowledge of self, their future spouse, and their relationship.
        e. Teach practical skills to help couples live what they promise.
E. Effects of the sacrament (CCC, nos. 1638-1642).
    1. Married couples are given the grace to love unselfishly.
    2. Also the grace to strengthen the permanent nature of their union and to appreciate the joy their union can bring (CCC, no. 1615).
    3. Couples are given the grace which strengthens them to attain eternal life (CCC, nos. 1617, 1639, 1641).
    4. When blessed with children, parents are helped to raise them in faith and love (CCC, nos. 1652-1654).
    5. Witness of faithful couples strengthens church community and the fabric of society (CCC, nos. 1655-1658).
F. Challenges to marriage and family life (CCC, nos. 1649-1651).
    1. Social challenges: acceptance of divorce and remarriage; popular cultural values are pushing aside traditional values; cohabitation before marriage; weakening of the bond between husband and wife.

    2. Increase in interchurch marriages.
    3. Impact of images in media, and challenges to traditional marriage in law.
    4. Blended families; loss of the extended family ties.
    5. Financial burdens; need for both parents to work outside the home.
    6. Loss of respect for the dignity of all human beings.
    7. Lack of willingness to accept children as a gift from God.
    8. Natural authority of parents is challenged.
  G. The question of divorce and/or remarriage.
    1. Christ teaches that a marriage lasts as long as both parties are still alive (CCC, no. 1650).
    2. When and why a civil divorce may be permitted (CCC, no. 1649).
      a. Civil divorce does not end a valid sacramental marriage.
      b. Sacraments for divorced but not remarried Catholics.
      c. Consequences for divorced Catholics who attempt marriage without a declaration of nullity (CCC, no. 1665).
        1) Catholic parties in a civil marriage are living in an objective state of sin; they are also a source of scandal to others.
        2) They are not separated from the Church and are obligated to attend Sunday Mass but are barred from the reception of sacraments except in danger of death.
        3) Ineligible to serve as a sponsor for Baptism or Confirmation.
    3. Determining the validity of previous marriage of divorced Catholics.
      a. A declaration of nullity of marriage can be issued if it is proven that there was a defect of consent, a defect of form, or the existence of an impediment (CCC, nos. 1625-1632).
      b. Other reasons for declaration of nullity.
        1) If one or both of the spouses lacked the psychological capacity to assume the essential obligations of marriage.
        2) If one or both were forced into the marriage.

IV. Sacrament of Holy Orders

  A. Instituted by Christ at the Last Supper as a sign of the Lord's abiding presence and priestly action in the Church (CCC, no. 1564).
  B. Historical development of the three orders of the sacrament.
    1. Apostles as the pastors and leaders of the early Church, the first bishops.
    2. As the Church grew, Apostles and successors ordained priests as their co-workers.
    3. Original deacons were ordained to serve material needs of community (Acts 6:1-7).
  C. The three degrees of Holy Orders.
    1. Bishop (office of sanctifying, teaching, and governing) (CCC, nos. 1555-1561).
      a. Successor of the Apostles.
      b. A member of the college of bishops in communion with pope.
      c. The bishop is the shepherd and high priest of a diocese, responsible for teaching and sanctifying his flock and proclaiming the truth to all; he wears a miter and carries a crozier to symbolize this.
      d. Bishop is understood as "married" to diocese; this is partly why he wears a ring.
      e. Minister of all sacraments.
        1) Confirmation generally conferred by bishops in the Latin Church.
        2) Ordination is reserved to bishops alone.
      f. Chosen by the pope from among priests.
      g. Archbishops and cardinals (or patriarch or major archbishop in some Eastern Churches).
    2. Priest (CCC, nos. 1562-1568).
      a. Priest acts in the person of Christ: *in persona Christi capitis*.
      b. Ordained by bishop as co-worker with bishop.
      c. Special focus of priest is ministry of the Word and of the sacraments.
      d. Generally serves in a parish; only a priest can serve as a pastor of a parish.
      e. Minister of:
        1) Sacraments of Baptism (and Chrismation in the Eastern Churches), Eucharist, Penance, Anointing of the Sick, and Confirmation in certain circumstances.
        2) In Sacrament of Marriage in the Latin Church, the priest receives the consent of the spouses in name of the Church and gives blessing of the Church (CCC, no. 1630).
    3. Deacon (CCC, nos. 1569-1571).
      a. Ordained by bishop to be of service to him and his priests.

b. Special focus of deacon is ministry of charitable service.
   c. Assists in celebration of the divine mysteries (CCC, no. 1570).
      1) Minister of Baptism (CCC, no. 1256).
      2) Assists at the Eucharist.
      3) Proclaims Gospel and preaches.
      4) Can preside at funerals.
      5) Assists at and blesses marriages (CCC, no. 1630).
   d. In the Eastern Churches the deacon is not the ordinary minister of Baptism and also cannot solemnize or witness a marriage.
   e. Types of deacons.
      1) Transitional: before being ordained a priest, a man is first ordained a deacon and serves in that role generally for six months to a year.
      2) Permanent: some men (including married men) are ordained deacons for life.
   4. Holy Orders is a sacrament reserved to men (CCC, no. 1577).
      a. "The Church has no authority whatsoever to confer priestly ordination on women" (OS, no. 4).
         1) It is not a question of the ability to carry out the functions of the ministry.
         2) It is the matter of what Christ has established, and the sacramental reality and symbolism of the priestly office.
      b. Bishop or priest serves as an icon of Christ: head of his Body, bridegroom of the Church.
      c. There is no historical basis for women serving as deacons in the diaconate as we now know and understand it.
D. Preparation.
   1. A bishop is prepared through ministry as a priest and through a life of prayer and sacrifice.
   2. Remote preparation for priesthood.
      a. As a child, there is the example of parish priests and the encouragement from family and community.
      b. Prayer and discernment by the candidate.
   3. A priest is prepared through years of formation in a seminary.
      a. Study of philosophy and theology.
      b. Human, intellectual, spiritual, and pastoral development.
      c. Understanding and embracing the promises he makes.
         1) Obedience to his bishop (CCC, no. 1567).
         2) The gift of celibacy; marriage renounced for the sake of the Kingdom (CCC, no. 1579).
         3) Priests in religious institutes must also embrace vows.
   4. A transitional deacon is prepared as part of his training for priesthood (CCC, nos. 1569-1571).
   5. Permanent deacons participate in a number of years of part-time preparation.
      a. Human and intellectual formation.
      b. Spiritual and pastoral formation.
E. Celebration of the sacrament.
   1. Essential element of each order is the laying on of hands by the bishop and the consecratory prayer (CCC, no. 1573).
   2. Chrism is used in the ordination of a priest and of a bishop (CCC, no. 1574).
      a. At the ordination of a priest, his hands are anointed with chrism.
      b. At the ordination of a bishop, chrism is poured on his head.
   3. Unique elements at the ordination of each.
      a. A bishop is presented with a ring, a crozier, and a miter.
      b. A priest is clothed in the vestments of a priest (stole and chasuble) and then is presented with the bread and wine that will be consecrated.
      c. A deacon is clothed in the vestments of a deacon (stole and dalmatic) and is presented with the *Book of the Gospels*, which he will proclaim.
F. Effects of the sacrament (CCC, nos. 1581-1584).
   1. The one ordained is marked with a permanent seal or character.
   2. Purpose of seal or character (CCC, nos. 1581-1584).

V. The Consecrated Life

A. The work of the Spirit in the various forms of consecrated life (CCC, nos. 914-933).
   1. Monastic life.
   2. The order of virgins; hermits and widows (CCC, nos. 920-924).
   3. Apostolic religious life (CCC, nos. 925-927).
   4. Secular institutes (CCC, nos. 928-929).
   5. Societies of apostolic life (CCC, no. 930).
   6. New expressions of consecrated life (CCC, nos. 931-933).

7. Lay ecclesial movements.
B. The evangelical counsels: poverty, chastity, and obedience (CCC, nos. 915-916).
C. Consecrated like Christ for the Kingdom of God.
D. The Paschal dimension of the consecrated life.
E. Witnesses to Christ in the world.
F. Eschatological dimension of the consecrated life.
G. The Virgin Mary, model of consecration and discipleship (CCC, nos. 967, 2030).

VI. Challenges

A. Isn't having the right vocation, job, or career essential for a person's happiness?
   1. No. The foundational call from God is not to a particular vocation, job, career, or way of life but to universal holiness and communion with him. This is the basis of all happiness.
   2. Often the key to happiness is using one's gifts fully for God by using them to serve others in Christian love.
   3. However, a refusal to answer God's call may result in a more difficult road to eternal life, or it may even jeopardize one's salvation.
B. Isn't the real measure of success in life the degree of one's financial security and material comfort?
   1. To some, the measure of success may be money and physical comforts, but that is not what Jesus Christ either taught or lived.
   2. Personal satisfaction in life finds a firm foundation in our relationship with the Lord and secondly in our relationships with other people.
   3. The ultimate goal in life should be holiness; this is where true success lies.
   4. In the Beatitudes, Jesus Christ teaches us attitudes essential for true happiness.
C. Just as people fall in love, they also fall out of love. Isn't a failed marriage just a regular part of life?
   1. Failed marriages might be a regular part of life, but they happen because of our fallen human nature. God teaches us to see and understand marriage as something which lasts for life.
   2. We know through Revelation that from the creation of the world and the creation of human beings, God's plan included marriage. Jesus Christ raised marriage to the level of a sacrament and taught that, properly understood, it involves lifelong commitment.
   3. Jesus Christ has taught us to recognize that the love between spouses is an image of the unending aspect of God's love for us; he has promised to love us, and he does not break his promises. Neither should we break promises of marriage.
   4. Married love involves not just feelings but also a commitment of reason and will; married love cannot deepen unless it faces and overcomes hard times and adversity.
   5. God does give the grace needed to live out our commitments.
D. Don't men and women who promise celibacy or lifelong chastity live lonely, unhappy lives?
   1. Some who promise lifelong celibacy and chastity may experience loneliness, as do some married people.
   2. Most men who become priests, monks, or brothers and most women who become nuns, sisters, and consecrated virgins generally live happy and fulfilling lives.
   3. Sexual intimacy with another is not essential for personal fulfillment and happiness.
   4. The heart of celibacy is a truly loving relationship with the Lord, expressed in a self-gift to others in his name.
   5. Committed celibacy for the sake of Jesus Christ and his Kingdom brings consolation that cannot be appreciated by one who has not lived it. Living a life of committed celibacy or chastity gives one a sense of the gifts of the eternal life to come.
   6. God gives the grace needed to live out our commitments.

Option E: Ecumenical and Interreligious Issues

The purpose of this course is to help the students understand the manner in which the Catholic Church relates to non-Catholic Christians as well as to other religions of the world. Building on the foundational truth that Jesus Christ established the Catholic Church and entrusted to her the fullness of God's Revelation, the course is intended to help students to recognize the ways in which important spiritual truths can also be found in non-Catholic Christian churches and ecclesial communities as well as in non-Christian religions. It is also intended to help them to recognize the ways in which other systems of belief and practice differ from the Catholic faith.

I. Revelation and the Catholic Church

A. Tracing Divine Revelation through the history of salvation.
  1. Divine Revelation in the Old Testament times.
      a. The Triune God is revealed in the work of Creation, which originates with the Father and is brought into being through the Word (Jesus Christ) by the power of the Holy Spirit (CCC, nos. 282, 314).
      b. God reveals himself to Abraham: the beginning of a people of faith (CCC, nos. 72, 992, 2571).
      c. In and through Abraham's descendents, he forms the People of Israel:
          1) Abraham's grandson, Jacob, has twelve sons whose descendants shape the twelve tribes of the People of Israel.
          2) "Israel" was the name given Jacob by God.
      d. God reveals himself to Moses and forms the People of Israel (CCC, nos. 62-64).
          1) He tells Moses about himself: "I am who am" (Ex 3:14).
          2) He gives the Israelites a code of both worship and morality.
  2. Divine Revelation in the New Testament (CCC, nos. 65-67, 124-127, 151, 422-455).
      a. In Jesus, the Eternal Word made man, is found the fullness of Revelation.
      b. Jesus is revealed as the Son of God and the Christ or "Anointed One" of God, the Messiah foretold by God through the prophets of Israel.
          1) The Annunciation to Mary (CCC, no. 494).
          2) Jesus' Baptism by St. John the Baptist (CCC, nos. 535-537).
          3) St. Peter's confession of faith at Caesarea Philippi (CCC, no. 552).
          4) Jesus' own proclamation of his divine Sonship (CCC, no. 590).
      c. Jesus reveals the Trinity, the central mystery of faith (CCC, nos. 648-650).
          1) Identifies himself as God's Son and addresses God as Father.
          2) Promises to send the Paraclete, the Holy Spirit.
          3) Sends the Holy Spirit upon the Apostles at Pentecost.
      d. Divine Revelation ends with the death of the last Apostle (CCC, nos. 66-67).

B. Divine foundation of the Catholic Church (CCC, nos. 758-769).
  1. Planned by God the Father from the beginning of time (CCC, no. 759).
  2. Pre-figured in the People of Israel (CCC, nos. 761-762).
  3. Divinely instituted by Jesus Christ, the Son of God and the Second Person of the Trinity (CCC, nos. 763-766).
  4. Revealed by the Holy Spirit (CCC, nos. 767-768).
  5. Guided, sustained, and sanctified by the Father through the Son and Holy Spirit (CCC, nos. 767-768).
  6. The Church is the Body of Christ; he is our Head, we are the members of the Body (CCC, nos. 790-795).

C. The Catholic Church and Divine Revelation.
  1. Jesus Christ instituted the Church on the foundation of the Apostles (CCC, nos. 857-860).
  2. The Apostles were entrusted with faithfully proclaiming the Gospel and spreading the Good News Jesus Christ had entrusted to them (CCC, no. 858).
  3. This role of ensuring an authentic proclamation of God's Revelation has been handed down in an unbroken line to the Apostles' successors—the pope and bishops (CCC, nos. 861-862).
  4. The Catholic Church, in and through the pope and the bishops, is entrusted with protecting the whole Deposit of Faith, that is, the Revelation preserved in Scripture and in Tradition (CCC, nos. 84, 863-865, 1202).

II. Christian Churches and Ecclesial Communities Apart from the Catholic Church

A. An ecclesiology of communion (CCC, nos. 787-789).
   1. Baptized people are in full communion with the Catholic Church when they are joined with Christ in the visible structure of the Church through the profession of faith, the reception of the sacraments, and respect and obedience toward those in authority in the Church (CIC, c. 205).
   2. Members of other Christian churches and ecclesial communities are in imperfect communion with the Catholic Church (CCC, nos. 836-838).
      a. The communion is imperfect because of differences in doctrine, discipline, and/or ecclesiastical structure.
      b. Christian churches (Orthodox Churches) are those with a validly ordained priesthood and the Eucharist (CCC, nos. 838).
      c. Christian ecclesial communities do not have a validly ordained priesthood or the Eucharist.
   3. The ecumenical movement works to overcome obstacles to full communion.
   4. All the baptized, including those in imperfect communion with the Catholic Church, are members of Christ's Body, have the right to be called Christian, and are brothers and sisters to members of the Catholic Church (UR, no. 3).

B. From the very beginning of the Church, there have been rifts and serious dissension (CCC, no. 817). Serious dissensions resulted in breaks from full communion with the Church.
   1. Schism with some Eastern Churches.
      a. Following the Council of Ephesus in 431.
         1) Because of a dispute over the title of Mary as Mother of God, some Churches, such as the Assyrian Church, broke away from full communion.
         2) Later some returned to union with Rome.
         3) Modern dialogue with those who did not return has made progress in healing this schism.
      b. Following the Council of Chalcedon in 451.
         1) Those who believed the Monophysite heresy (that Jesus did not have both a divine nature and a human nature) also broke away from full communion with the Church and formed what are called the Oriental Orthodox Churches.
         2) Modern dialogue with the Oriental Orthodox Catholics has made progress in healing this schism.
   2. The Catholic Church and the Eastern Orthodox Church were one until 1054.
      a. The Schism of 1054 resulted in the establishment of the Eastern Orthodox Churches.
      b. Contributing causes to the Schism of 1054.
         1) *Filioque* controversy (CCC, nos. 247-248).
         2) Growing cultural and political differences between East and West.
         3) Different forms of Church governance emerged.
            a) Eastern Churches were governed by synods with a patriarch.
            b) Latin Church was monarchical with the pope as final authority.
      c. Difference between Orthodox Churches and Eastern Catholic Churches.
         1) They share the same liturgy but not the same bonds of episcopal communion.
      d. Orthodox Churches and Catholic Church have strong ties to each other.
         1) Same core doctrine, beliefs, and moral teachings.
         2) Both have Apostolic Succession.
         3) Seven sacraments, validity of ordinations.
      e. Differences between the Catholic Church and Eastern Orthodox Churches.
         1) Most significant: Orthodox Churches do not recognize the infallibility or the primacy of jurisdiction of the Pope.
         2) A few doctrinal formulations in the liturgy: the Eastern Orthodox Churches use the original wording of the Nicene Creed and do not accept the addition of the *filioque* (the Holy Spirit proceeds from the Father and the Son).
         3) Differences in sacramental law and practice (e.g., Orthodox tolerate divorce and remarriage).
         4) Some Marian dogmas are taught in a different way.
         5) Ecumenical councils: not all accepted by the Orthodox Churches.
   3. Ecclesial communions: Anglican (Episcopalian), Lutheran, Reformed Christian.
      a. Who founded these various ecclesial communities and why?
      b. Common ties between the Catholic Church and these ecclesial communions.

1) Common beliefs about Christ derived from Scripture.
2) Baptisms celebrated with the Trinitarian formula and proper intention are considered valid by the Catholic Church.
3) In many cases, common moral convictions.
4) Some common liturgical practices, e.g., common cycle of Scripture readings.

   c. Differences.
   1) Differences in acceptance of the authority of the pope.
   2) Differences in doctrine, e.g., Calvinist belief in predestination.
   3) Differences in sacramental economy and practice, particularly the lack of the Sacrament of Holy Orders and, consequently, of a valid Eucharist.
   4) Differences on moral questions: e.g., abortion, divorce, and remarriage.

4. Other Christian communities.
   a. Some are the result of further divisions among ecclesial communions which separated from the Catholic Church, e.g., Methodists separated from the Anglican Church.
   b. Shared belief in Christ and the Triune God but a strong emphasis on *sola Scriptura* (Scripture alone) as the standard for determining belief.
   c. Differences in doctrine, sacramental understanding and practice, morality.
   d. Many of these bodies (e.g., Baptists, Congregationalists) view the church as a local congregation and not a worldwide communion.

C. Ecumenical efforts.
   1. Ecumenism involves efforts aimed at fostering unity between the Catholic Church and other churches and Christian ecclesial communities.
   2. Ecumenical activity requires the following (CCC, no. 821):
      a. Renewal of the Catholic Church in fidelity to her vocation.
      b. Conversion of heart by all the faithful.
      c. Prayer in common where appropriate.
      d. Fraternal knowledge of each other.
      e. Ecumenical formation of clergy and laity (knowledge of sacred theology including a historical perspective; understanding of the problems and benefits of the ecumenical movement).
      f. Dialogue among theologians of different churches and communities.
      g. Collaboration in activities of service to others.
   3. Greater hope of restoring full communion where there is
      a. A visible continuity with the ancient Church (Apostolic Succession).
      b. A shared understanding of interpreting revealed truth (Scripture read through the lens of Tradition), e.g., such a starting point exists with the Orthodox Churches.
      c. Practice of the sacraments.
   4. Greater obstacles continue to arise in doctrine and in praxis: e.g., ecclesial communions allowing women and non-celibate homosexuals to serve as ordained ministers.

III. The Relationship of the Catholic Church to the Jewish People

A. The link between the Catholic Church and the Jewish people is special.
   1. Pope John Paul II referred to the Jewish people as "our elder brothers."
   2. The Jewish people were God's special choice to be the instrument for the salvation of the world. They were the first to hear the Word of God, that is, Divine Revelation (CCC, no. 839).

B. The relationship between the Catholic Church and the Jewish people holds a unique and special position.
   1. Unlike other non-Christian religions, the Jewish faith is a response to God's Revelation in the Old Covenant (CCC, no. 839).
   2. The patriarchs of the Jewish people—Abraham, Isaac, Jacob, and Moses—are also the ancestors in faith for members of the Catholic Church.
   3. The Jewish people are the original Chosen People of God; Christians are the new People of God (CCC, no. 840).
   4. Our Savior, Jesus Christ, was born and raised as a Jew. Mary, the Apostles, and the disciples were also Jews.
   5. The New Covenant with Jesus Christ is the fulfillment of the promises of the first Covenant between God and the Jewish people.
   6. Catholics and Jews share common elements of moral life and practice:

  a. The Decalogue is a strong part of Catholic moral teaching and tradition.
  b. Jesus Christ drew on the Decalogue and the teaching of the prophets in his teaching on self-giving love and moral living.
 C. Fundamental differences with the Catholic Church.
  1. The Jewish people do not acknowledge Jesus as a Divine Person, the Son of God, or the promised Messiah, nor do they accept the revealed truth of the Triune God, which is what is unique to Christian Revelation.
  2. The Jewish people have no sacramental economy; they continue to rely on the ritual prescriptions of the first Covenant reinterpreted for post-Temple Judaism.
 D. Anti-Judaism or anti-Semitism was evident among Catholics for many centuries.
  1. The Catholic Church condemns all unjust discrimination, including anti-Semitism.
  2. In the twentieth century, the Catholic Church dropped from its liturgy any inference that the Jewish people as a whole were responsible for the Death of Christ because the truth is that the sins of all humanity were the cause of his Death.
 E. Dialogue with the Jewish people.
  1. This dialogue has a unique character in that we share roots of faith.
  2. This dialogue also has an interfaith character because of the differences in faith and in sacramental understanding and practice.
  3. Aims of this dialogue include
   a. Grow in mutual respect for one another as sons and daughters of God.
   b. Give common witness on matters of peace and justice.
   c. Deepen mutual understanding of the one God and his plan for the world.
   d. Bring all to Jesus Christ and to his Church (Rom 11:12, 15, 25; CCC, nos. 674, 1043).

IV. The Church and Other Non-Christians

 A. The Muslim people.
  1. Monotheistic (but non-Trinitarian) faith in common with Jews and Christians.
  2. The Catholic Church and Muslims acknowledge God as the Creator and claim ties to the faith of Abraham.
  3. The Muslim people do not acknowledge God as the Father of Jesus, or Jesus Christ as the Divine Son of God, nor do they accept the Triune God, but they do revere Jesus as a prophet and Mary as the Virgin Mother of Jesus.
  4. There are many common elements of moral life and practice between Catholics and Muslims.
  5. Islam has no sacramental economy; Islamic law requires testimony of faith, prayer, fasting, almsgiving, and pilgrimage as expressions of faith.
  6. Unlike the Catholic Church, Islam has no central figure of authority on matters of faith and morals; there are also different ways to interpret the Qur'an.
  7. The Crusades and their lasting impact.
  8. The Catholic Church seeks to engage the Muslim community in dialogue to advance human solidarity.
 B. There are non-Christian religions common in the United States, including major world religions such as Hinduism and Buddhism, and others such as Sikhs, Mormons, and Bahai.
  1. Common elements with Christianity.
   a. As human beings we share a common origin and end.
   b. Many of these religions teach to some degree compassionate action, moral restraint, spiritual discipline, and respect for human dignity.
   c. These religions contain elements of truth and virtue, which can help orient their members toward reception of the Gospel.
  2. Those who do not know Christ but who still strive to know and live in truth and holiness can be saved.
  3. The fulfillment of the values and virtues of other religions is found in what the Catholic Church proclaims:
   a. God is one, and that God is Triune.
   b. Jesus Christ as the Son of God.
   c. Salvation is a gift of grace available through faith in Jesus Christ.
   d. Sanctification is for human beings to participate in the love of God now and eternally.

V. Proclamation and Dialogue

 A. The Catholic Church possesses the fullness of the means of salvation willed by God as the ordinary way of saving all people.
  1. "All salvation comes from Christ the Head through the Church which is his Body" (CCC, no. 846).
   a. God is one and that God is Triune.

  b. Jesus Christ as the Son of God.
  c. Salvation is a gift of grace available through faith in Jesus Christ.
  d. Sanctification is for human beings to participate in the love of God now and eternally.
 2. "Those who, through no fault of their own, do not know the Gospel of Christ or his Church, but who nevertheless seek God with a sincere heart, and, moved by grace, try in their actions to do his will as they know it through the dictates of their conscience—those too may achieve eternal salvation" (CCC, no. 847; LG, no. 16).
 3. "'Although in ways known to himself God can lead those who, through no fault of their own, are ignorant of the Gospel, to that faith without which it is impossible to please him, the Church still has the obligation and also the sacred right to evangelize all men'" (CCC, no. 848; LG, no. 16).

B. Interreligious dialogue.
 1. There are many forms of interreligious dialogue.
  a. The dialogue of daily life in religiously pluralistic societies/communities.
  b. The dialogue of shared service to the needy.
  c. The dialogue of theologians and scholars.
  d. The dialogue of shared spiritual experience.
 2. Such dialogue requires mutual search for truth among those learned in their own religious traditions.
 3. Requires respect and understanding of differences in culture as well as in belief.
 4. Requires training in accurate knowledge of other religions.
 5. Can and should involve working together in service to those in need.

VI. Challenges

A. Isn't one faith or religion just as good as any other?
 1. No, that statement is not true. The fullness of Revelation and truth subsists in the Catholic Church.
 2. If one has been given the gift of faith and chooses to reject or neglect that gift, that person acts in a way that is gravely wrong.
 3. The Church engages in many types of dialogue, both ecumenical and interfaith. Those dialogues are characterized by respect and aim to bring about more unity.

B. Isn't it more important to show tolerance and not say that the Catholic faith is better than any other?
 1. Judgment about the truth of the Catholic faith does not mean that Catholics should not show respect toward people of other faiths and religions.
 2. Respect involves the effort of mutual respect and charity, and a refusal to treat one as less worthy because of differences.
 3. Catholics are to be respectful of people in their intrinsic dignity but not tolerant of falsehood.

C. If unity of people in faith is the real goal, why can't each side compromise?
 1. While unity of Christians is an important goal, the Catholic Church cannot compromise on the truth of what God has revealed. Truth is one; we need to subject ourselves to the whole truth.
 2. Where there are intrinsic contradictions in belief, one belief is true and one must be false.
 3. Sometimes, however, we overemphasize some aspects of the truth at the expense of other aspects. Serious, respectful, and loving pursuit of the whole truth can help us recapture the needed balance.

D. What caused the four divisions in Christianity from the time of Ephesus, Chalcedon, the Schism of 1054, and the Protestant Reformation? Is there any hope of unity?
 1. There were various reasons for the divisions.
  a. In each case, there were disagreements about doctrine.
  b. In each case, some degree of politics also contributed to the fractures.
 2. Since Vatican II, the Catholic Church has initiated and sponsored many meetings and dialogues with hope for movement toward unity. Positive outcomes include the following:
  a. A willingness to meet face to face for prayer and dialogue.
  b. Occasional joint statements on matters of doctrine and belief (e.g., joint statement with Anglicans on Mary, joint statement with Lutherans on justification).